MEMORY PALACE

How to Remember Everything You Learn

(Improvement Techniques to Maximize Your
Memory Capacity)

Royal Massey

Published By Royal Massey

Royal Massey

Memory Palace: How to Remember Everything You Learn (Improvement Techniques to Maximize Your Memory Capacity)

ISBN 978-1-77485-417-4

Legal & Disclaimer

TABLE OF CONTENTS

Introduction

Imagine a world without memories (that's quite difficult, isn't it?). The thing I want you to do is to suppose that you are unable to recall the details of your childhood or that of you had a high school buddy, the topic you discussed with a colleague yesterday and the list goes on. The fact is that memories are the core for our lives. It is the basis of your identity and it impacts every part of life!

The fact that memory is an essential aspect of our existence cannot be understated. As soon as an individual reaches the age that he or she is aware of their activities, their memory is vital. The ability to manage memory and to recall important details is essential to your individual productivity, success and growth in all tasks. In the constant process of forgetting discussions from the meeting, and needing to review a specific memo time and again is inefficient and time-consuming.

You are what you are today due to your incredible memory. Imagine that you've no memory, and I come to you and request that you introduce yourself. It would be a good idea to think about in order for the sake of introducing yourself. Your memory functions as an electronic storage system in which all your personal information is stored. Without memory you will not be able to make progress, think or possess intelligence.

We live in an information age , where nearly every piece of information you require is accessible via an Google search. However regardless the fact that you need vital information that is readily available. It is not a good idea to risk the shame of needing to consult manuals and notes throughout the course of your job as it can make appearance unprofessional. It can be time-consuming and ineffective. A lack of memory can result in poor judgement.

To make your life better You must improve your memory. A healthy memory enhances the potential of your natural abilities and abilities because you are able to get information quickly and quickly. A better memory also implies an increase in intelligence because intelligence is the ability to remember information and information. You've got a remarkable memory that is able to improve regardless of the level of your memory today. Be assured that your memory and brain can be unlimited.

Some students achieve better results than others because they have more retentive memory than other students. There are those who believe that certain people are naturally intelligent and brilliant. Although that may be true however, one's memory could be improved. You'll be amazed by the results of a few exercise to improve memory. These results are evidence for the idea that memory improvement is possible.

This book , 'developing an excellent Memory' will show readers in easy clear and concise ways, how human memory functions as well as the different elements that affect memory positively and negatively, and how you can use this knowledge to boost your memory to a degree that is sure to surprise you. I won't overly burden you with postulations, theories, and hypotheses; instead, I'll be straightforward and concrete.

A few of us have weak observation skills - we're not attentive and passive. We could glance at our watch but not be able to tell when exactly it is while others are unable to remember what the names of place that we frequent. It's a party and, when you're presented to another one, you realise you've already forgot your name. initial person you've met. Have you ever waited around for the chance to make a statement at an event, and when it's finally your turn you realize that you've forgotten the exact words you were planning to say? This could be a sign of poor memory abilities since a great memory is when you are able to recall details quickly at any time. But, don't think you can recall information that you didn't pay any time to. We are all poor listeners, which is why we tend to forget fast.

It is important to remember that the first step in developing better memory is paying to your surroundings (in another words, observe!).

There isn't a memory enhancement medication or a single method to bring an immediate improvement in memory. There are a variety of variables that impact memory such as motivation, interest as well as health etc. will be taken care of.

My primary goals in this book is to give you the best tips and tricks to allow you to be a master at recall and memory in the process. Also, to keep your brain healthy and strong. So , sit back and relax as we embark on this easy journey.

Chapter 1: The Memory Palace

1. Pick a location or area that you are comfortable with. This could be your home or areas of your home or at school, or even an your office. It's your choice. You should have at minimum 12 memory locations like your living space, the front yard, the garden patio, pool. It doesn't matter which one you decide to choose, as long as it's something is familiar to you and that you quickly associate with a specific term or phrase you'll need to remember.

2. Shut your eyes, and picture the space. Make a mental picture of the space you are in and gradually become used to it. There is a region of the brain that is able to remember spatial locations that is known as the hippocampal area. It aids in remembering locations you've visited and, as a result, you'll be able to quickly recall the place that you were raised in or the place you played when you were a child. Spatial memory is awe-inspiring.

3. Let's say you're going on an excursion to buy five groceries. Also, take the items you'll need and then break it into pieces.

4. If you are in the situation of having to purchase 5 groceries then follow this procedure. Before you head out to the supermarket follow these steps:

Imagine that one of the items you'll need to buy includes cottage cheese. Imagine that you are driving down the driveway and you spot an enormous bowl of the cottage cheese blocking your path. Imagine it as smelly and old. Think of this item as having an unpleasant smell and a large tub.

5. the cereal box. If you open your front door, you will see hundreds of cereal boxes are awaiting you at your front yard. If you head to the supermarket, think of the cereal boxes that are in your front garden. Then, you can open the box and you will see serial numbers appearing. This is how you'll remember purchasing a box cereal.

The next thing on the list is bananas. Imagine in your hallway, and you suddenly see Frank Sinatra singing to a huge banana that is parked across the hall. To make the scene more fascinating, imagine Frank Sinatra wearing a Speedo while he sings to this banana. This is something you should remember!

The next item to be purchased is a box of cookies. Take a look around your living space and you will see a huge cookie baking on top of your TV. The bag heats up and the TV melts right in the front of your eyes.

The last thing is to have a head lettuce. Imagine an entire head of lettuce sitting over your refrigerator inside the kitchen. Imagine the lettuce having legs and arms. It's screaming at you to not use it in cooking.

6. Now that you have completed all that, you're ready to go to the supermarket Imagine your home. Imagine you are entering the driveway and see the huge bowl of cottage cheese. You go towards

the front door where cereal bags are. As you walk through the front door , you will notice the huge banana, with Frank Sinatra in a Speedo singing in the hallway. Then you look at the cookie bag melt on the TV set as you look into the kitchen, you can see an oversized lettuce head, with legs and arms shouting at you.

You can apply this method to memorize anything you'll need to remember.

Chapter 2: Create Images More Relevant

The method described within this section was meant to aid one in memorizing Bible verses. The method involves creating images that are able to be correlated with the Bible verses you'll need to remember, however you'll also have to make them more appealing so that you will be able to easily recall the verses.

1. Learn whatever you have to learn then "anchor" that to something you're already familiar with.

Take a deep breath and close your eyes. Begin by entering the memory palace. Imagine yourself walking out of your front door . As you open the door you can see a huge anchor at the center of your back yard. Imagine yourself leaping up and rising until you reach the top. When you are there take a look around to find the objects you recognize like your homes of friends and churches, structures and other landmarks.

Then look toward the grass in your front yard, and you can see a huge plasma television, as big as a pool. You can jump and dive into it.

2. Place yourself in the image and connect to the image.

A splash in the huge pool gives you an image that is new. You don't have to be the one doing the jumping. Visit your mind's palace and associate in the same room as the person performing all the tasks. This makes your memory more private.

The moment you jumped into the water you came to an enormous stream in your backyard. It is there that you can witness John the Baptist Baptizing Jesus Christ. While you watch as John is the Baptist is baptizing Jesus the Christ, you hear a man yell"Act! You glanced around and you was able to see Dracula with an older camera and filming the entire scene.

3. Your images must be animated.

To give it a unique look The images must be moving in the manner they should. This will lead our attention to the following stage:

4. Your images should be more crazy and more weird.

There is nothing more crazy than the inclusion of Dracula present in the moment when Jesus is Baptized in the name of John The Baptist! When you hear Dracula perform his actions think about the possibility that you smell his breath. And since he's an undead vampire, his breath is disgusting.

5. Engage all possible of your sensory systems as you can.

In addition, you can smell the breath of Dracula, listen to Dracula and John the Baptist speak and be able to feel the time.

6. Inject your emotions.

The purpose of this method is to be fully present, so you are able to see as well as hear and feel. Check out what the scene is doing to you feel. Are you feeling excited, sad, or happy or sad? Bring those emotions into your brain

7. Take a look at the picture from a different perspective.

Imagine yourself leaping across the opposite part of the river. Now you can see the world from a different angle. Take a look at Dracula with the camera. Also, look at John as the Baptist as well as Jesus. While you are present in the scene you are part of the scene. Imagine yourself dressed as the character of a prophet or Moses.

8. Note it down.

Imagine yourself holding stones and an axe in your hands. You will hear John the Baptist saying to be the sole witness to this incident aside from Dracula. He advised you to record what you saw and so you picked up the chisel, and began carving into the tablets of stone. Watch Jesus emerge from the water and He instructed you to inform all the people around you about this historic incident.

9. Tell us what you know.

When you were listening to Jesus speak, you've leapt into the river. Now, you are moving towards the home. You've opened the front door and your family members see you dressed like prophetic, with a beard, hair that is long, and worn-out clothing.

Retell the story you observed to your family and friends. This is the way you'll be able to recall all the details. When you talk about your notes and it is engraved in your mind.

10. Listen to and record.

As soon as you start talking about what you've seen the wife pulls out the tape recorder and starts recording your conversation. After you've finished recording, you can continue the recording repeatedly.

The 10 tips listed here are simple to follow. Always begin at the beginning of your Memory Palace. This can be used for various ways. If you're a student, it is a great way to help you learn your lessons or, if you're an educator, you could make use of this to aid students in remembering things.

Chapter 3: The Major System

The memory of numbers isn't easy. It's a fact that the brain is unable to recall abstract concepts such as emotions and numbers. The most effective method to remember is to transform a collection number into something that you already know, such as the guitar or sailing boat.

Take the numbers from 0-9 and assign a phonetic sound for each one of them.

0 0. S, C, Z

1 T 1 - D

2 N

3 - M

4 - R

5 - 5 -

6 6 CH, SH, J

7. G, K and C (hard C like in color)

8 - F 8 - F

9 9 P 9 - P

To help you remember them, you can associate it with the various parts of your body , starting with your feet. Imagine your body and place an identifier to a specific body part.

1. S to the the sole of the feet, or T for the toes

2. Go until your knees (has an N sound when it is pronounced)

3. Continue to move towards the muscles of the legs and M for the muscles

4. You have are now at your rear

5 - Starting from the rear, you reach your stomach region where you will find love handles 5 L

6 - Shoulder, chest, and joints

7 7 Greyson Kit Carl (you can make this one any way you want but this could be include the names of your children)

8 Face

9 - Pupil is in your brain, eyes

Pick any number, call the phone number and then write the numbers. Note how vowels are absent. You will be using them to form phrases and words.

Example Dark fur chap on an American cowboy.

D=1 R=4 K=7 F=8 R=4 Ch=6 P=9 N=2 C=0 B=9

1-4-7-8-4-6-9-2-0-9

It could be a telephone number. Try this out when you're within your mind palace. It's more efficient.

Chapter 4: Be Good at Recalling People

It's common for people to lose names and names, especially in the case of meeting been introduced to someone for the very first time. It's embarrassing when you meet someone who is familiar to you , but you are unable to remember their name.

It is possible to use this in conjunction in conjunction with other methods, such as the memory place system and the major system.

To demonstrate:

Just met a guy known as Baker which is not uncommon to forget. If you meet again, and you didn't remember his name. It is not possible to say hello to Herr. Baker, because you were introduced, so you ought to be acquainted with each one another.

The best way to approach this is to associate his name with an object that you are familiar with, something that you used to know. Imagine him as a real baker.

Imagine him wearing a large headdress, covered with flour, while holding a baked bread loaf. Imagine the aroma of cake and make it a part of your imagination. If you ever meet this person again you'll be able to imagine the image of a bakery, and you'll be able to tell he's the Mr. Baker.

Remember the concept of memorizing something , and then convert it into information you know to a format that is familiar to you.

Chapter 5: Memorize Every Day

"In each day, we have 1,440 minutes. That's 1440 chances to have an impact."

~ Les Brown

If you're looking to have the ability to remember things with ease by practicing daily, it can be helpful. It's easy; you must have an item to remember every single day.

Why do you need to remember this every single day? Here are three rational reasons:

Every day, you should be able to remember. It's similar to exercising your muscles; it keeps your brain "geared". This is the same reasoning that a professional footballer must practice even in off seasons. While it is true that he may not practice, it doesn't mean the player doesn't have the abilities, but he'll be ineffective and slow to get back into form when the season begins.

It's possible that following an exhausting day of practice after a long offseason or after a game without the advantage of practicing and feeling exhausted the next day. The ability are there forever, but without consistent practice, it can be difficult to achieve your brain "functioning" as it ought to.

* Vocabulary development is tied to speed and consistency. The more frequently you are practicing memorizing, and the faster you work, the more connections you'll make in addition to the fact that you will benefit from these connections to communicate your message using the language and be able to comprehend the meaning of what you read and hear. This will also motivate you to continue practicing and produce better outcomes. When you are more consistent you improve your creativity, allowing you to produce more vibrant pictures.

Every day practice increases the amount of time you can retain your vocabulary as high as 100 percent.

If you're speaking in your native language it's a normal circumstance to not find the correct words every say the right thing every day. It's normal to lose a few words every now and then and especially when you can't discover the right words to use. But, you don't require to always know the correct words. You simply need to practice and enter the memory park (from the beginning chapter) more frequently.

Are you a college student but aren't able to commit the time to learning words from a certain word, don't be concerned since there are plenty of other methods to test your memorization abilities. It is possible to use this method to remember random numbers or dates, or even randomized cards.

Simple Strategies to Apply

1. You can ask your friends or a random person about their birthday date and keep it in mind.

2. When you go for a grocery shop or dine at a restaurant you should ask the cashier their name. You can then remember their number.

3. While you shop for groceries Make a note of the cost of each item as you add them to the shopping basket. Bonus points are awarded when you have them arranged in your head as you recall the prices of every item.

4. Are you looking for something to do traveling? Take a look at the license plates and keep them in mind.

5. Here's a method that works Walk around the neighborhood , or visit the subdivision nearby and remember every street's name. This is a great exercise for you to do too.

6. It's a simple process by listening to music, and then memorize the lyrics. For those who love music, this is simple because the repetition of a song and over can help them remember the lyrics. This is an effective and efficient method to help your brain to be working.

7. Take out your mobile and find the cellular number of the most important person in your life and keep it in mind. You probably don't remember the number of

your sister's cell phone. Since you've become comfortable with the speed dialing feature on your phone, you'll not even keep track of the phone numbers of those you talk to frequently.

8. While you wait to board your bus stop, or as you wait for your food to be served in restaurants, be sure to note down the ingredients in the soda you drink. Note their quantities should you need to.

9. At the bus stop, or at the station for trains, remember the timetable of the bus you typically take to and from work.

10. If you are on the bus or train take note of the color of the clothes from the very first 10 persons that you encounter when you're looking for seats.

There are a variety of exercises that are simple and can incorporate into your daily routines or other things. Certain of them are quantitative, but others aren't. The great thing about practicing regularly will improve your accuracy along with your speed and ability to think on your feet. If you are able to take a seat and go through your textbook in preparation in preparation for the exam, you brain will be working in a way that helps you are able to easily remember and remember the details you require.

Don't forget that if your don't work your brain, it'll be weakened and you'll discover it difficult to remember things.

Chapter 6: Remember the Chapters in your textbook, Ace the Test

"Nice intro quote here..." ~ Someone famous

It would be amazing to be able to remember the contents of textbooks and pass the exam in that area? It may seem impossible, however it's actually possible and you can be able to learn more about the subject within this section.

Before beginning each step listed below start with your Memory Palace (discussed in the first chapter).

Now, go to work.

1. Start with the book and go through the end.

When you read an ebook in the very first instance, take your time to look at the front and back covers. Start by reading the colophon first, then the table content, the introduction and concluding paragraph, and finally, look through the index (if there is one). The pages that are not in the book are referred to as "paratext" and the "text that is placed next to the text. The term was used by scholar Gerrard Genette.

The process should take about five minutes. The brain benefits from this because it is able to effectively help it comprehend the nature of the book in relationship to its subject.

The conclusion is also included since it can be used to check to see if the conclusion made by the author regarding his or her subject was sufficiently profound that it warrants reading all the steps required to reach the conclusion. The introduction as well as the conclusion will provide information to the chapter of the book you ought to be focusing on.

2. Index card tools.

Find an index card and note down the name of the author and the book's title and the entire bibliographical details. Then, label this as card "1" on the top left corner on an index card. Before you begin reading, you will be able to choose ahead of time on the number of pieces of information you wish to learn from it. This is called"predetermination" or the "principle of prior determination". It is possible to set a default of three specifics for each chapter. You can add more details should you wish.

This is the reason you are doing this:

Inability to plan is in fact making plans to fall, especially in the case of planned reading.

* Predetermination will ensure that you do not get overwhelmed.

Be aware that less is better. It's not logical to overwhelm your brain with a lot of facts. Concentrating on the most important aspects can be more efficient when learning.

3. Now is the time to start.

If you've studied and comprehended the introduction and conclusion, you should have an idea of the chapters to be focusing on. Begin by reading the chapters you've identified.

4. Consider thinking in "3s".

In this stage you've got three details that you will learn from a specific chapter. Make your index cards available even if you only numbered one card and you must be ready to write on the card.

5. Establish an expectation of ownership.

Make a habit of being aware of the main information contained in the book. If the book becomes boring then you can opt to "play an game". Imagine that you are the anchor of your own talk-show, and you'll be able to talk with the author. You are aware that millions of viewers will be watching, therefore it is crucial to gather plenty of information about the book. Therefore, you must go through the book as quickly as you can.

This method lets you ask questions while you are reading. This will stimulate your curiosity as you are actively engaged with the writing portion. It is possible to pretend that the author is in the middle of you and answering your questions, but in this instance you're imagining what the responses of the author will be.

6. Categorize. It's a game of numbers.

When you discover something important, make sure you note it down on an index card. Include the page number in the top right corner. You can do this without not jotting down a quotation in the text. This allows you to return to the data whenever you require it. If you have other ideas, write them down in the bottom on the index card.

It is not necessary to be pressured into learning any information. The key is familiarizing rather than learning. It's about connecting the specifics to the knowledge you already have.

Perhaps you've read a 10 chapter book and have three index cards per chapter. Each index card is a numbers, and all of them. It is necessary to create 30 stations for your brain's palace.

7. Begin memorizing.

Next, start with the number 1 card. It is crucial to remember the title and name of the writer.

8. Make use of the author's book to create a visual representation.

It is possible to use the author as an "bridging character" to travel from one location to another. It is possible to find photos of the author on the internet and then connect it to something familiar before moving from there.

9. Exaggerate.

Create large, bold colorful, bright and exciting pictures about the book. The bigger the pictures are, the more impressive.

10. Do a test first.

The final step is to check whether you can remember what you have to learn. This will ensure that the facts are stored in your brain and this is the proof that you were capable of retaining everything.

Chapter 7: Memory Palace: The Essentials

What is it?

A Greco-Roman technique called 'Memory Palace is a technique that allows you to use the physical structure of things in order to transform memories, impressions and recollections into permanent memory placeholders for your brain. These memories are stored in physical places within a particular arrangement that you decide to use.

When you move your brain through a particular arrangement, you can connect the hanging pieces into an unified tapestry filled with vivid imagery which allows your brain to remember and recall, leading to what we call"good memory.".

History and the Use Of Memory Palace

The Memory Palace is an process that is also referred to as the Roman Room"mind palace" or the'method for loci'.

The things that are remembered using this mnemonic system are linked to specific physical places known as loci. Loci is an Latin word that means "places," and it is utilized in early rhetorical Greek treatises (Cicero's De Oratore, Rhetorica in Herennium, as well as Quintilian's Instituteo Oratoria). The method relies on spatial connections that are memorized to construct an organized, logical, and organize content that must be retained. By intense visualization, like you were actually in the imaginary area, data becomes more easy to find. The more intensive you visualize, the more easily accessible information will be at a later date.

Grand Masters of Memory, people who have earned the title through participating in memory contests they claim to utilize the technique of the memory palace to recall faces, digits and the words that appear in lists.

They do not believe that their achievements are due to an obscure and arrogant claim of'superior intelligence' or "innate abilities Instead, they all-of-a-while attribute their success to their use of the subject matter in this book the memory palace technique.

Chapter 8: Memory Techniques

Memory Palaces And Images

Memory Palace

Follow this guideline to create an memory palace:

1. Choose a Building and Follow a Specific Way

First of all, what exactly is an memory aid? A mnemonic can be anything that you use to aid in recalling other things. For instance, the phrase "Never Eat Soggy Waffles" is a mnemonic that helps to remember the cardinal directions of North, East, South and West. This phrase throughout the remainder of this book.

When selecting the perfect memory palace, it is important to select a one that you're familiar with well. More familiar are you with this place (building or the outdoor area, home the likes of.) The more details you are able to precisely store and recall in this memory palace.

Then, choose a route within the space that you are familiar with. It could be your way through the bathroom until your bedroom, or from the time you get up until the time you go to work. Recognize the seemingly insignificant details. Like the peeling paint on the ceiling's corner or the bathroom floor which always appears to be uneven or the tile's color which you're unable to recognize.

2. You can arrange your ideas in a sequence across the Palace

For example, if you have to think of the names of your friends who are going to an event, imagine that you must leave your home and your best friend is waiting in front of the door. the second one is locked in a pot near the bottom of your driveway needing assistance; and the third working in the kitchen trying to make cookies to take along (you already know the friend who's never late). Integrate their distinct qualities into the narrative to enhance the story's impact.

You can easily recall ideas by arranging them in the memory palace. It could include important components in a presentation, list of grocery items, even your book contents. You must think about every space in the memory palace. then come up with your own components (you can do this mentally or create a list using illustrations) and connect them to a particular location.

The link you create between your idea and place should be simple to keep in mind. For example, in the example above, incorporating your friends' real personality characteristics in the story can make it easier for you to remember the story later on.

The most important thing to remember is to be creative enough to think of the mnemonic you are able to visualize as an incredibly rich animation, or image. The more sensory elements you can incorporate (i.e. hearing, smell, touch and taste, as well as observe) the easier it becomes to keep in mind. For instance, how could you possibly forget your best acquaintance if they're the first person you encounter after leaving the house. You will initially encounter resistance due to the fact that remembering human-made objects that do not pose an immediate danger to our survival isn't in line with our evolutionary past. This means that there is an initial obstacle that you must overcome. If it was simple to remember everything the majority of people would be able to do it. Be aware of the challenges as, ultimately, that's what differentiates you from those who just go through this book but do nothing but read it and.

Retrace Your Route

To be able to recall all your acquaintances it is necessary to follow your steps through the memory palace that you have created. Track your steps all through at the entrance of your home to the neighbor in the kitchen, imagining every spot in the building while you think of your buddies.

Images

Although there aren't any studies which have proved the existence of "photographic memories' the truth is that all of us have "photographic memories". The human brain is best at working by using pictures.

You are probably familiar with this game of memorization, in which you must study the image over a specified duration of time, which is usually one minute, and then you will be asked questions about the information contained in the image.

Let's look at an example from this image:

You can take a moment to look at this picture.

As ridiculous and innocent as it may seem take a look at the following possible questions that could be asked about the image:

* How many children in the photo are screaming?

What number of boats could you spot in the picture?

* There's a structure visible in the picture. Is it a church house, water tower or tent?

The number is a bit confusing. How many ducks could you see in the picture?

* Is there a child in the photo dressed in green?

There's a child in the center of the picture with a printed image of his shirt. Is it a pentagon square, star, or the crescent?

* What's the color of the sky that appears in this image?

In spite of its simple nature, there is an astonishing number of factors to keep in mind. Here are some tips you can follow to break down the dose of stimuli into small pieces of information that you can later remember.

1. Divide the image into segments

In the beginning, you must split or divide the image into 5-10 segments or pieces. For that image you could divide it into five segments:

1. Mountain ranges in background

2. The blue sky

3. The river

4. This is the right-hand side right shore of the river.

5. Left side of left shore of the

The next step is to develop a mnemonic for each of these places. You could, for instance, link these sections or pieces to a place that is familiar in Your memory palace. This could be done as follows:

1. The Mountains - The bedroom of your parents

2. The Sky is your bedroom ceiling

3. The river is in your bathroom

4. Right Shore - Your kitchen

5. Left Shore - Your laundry room

2. Remember

Once you've developed the mnemonics which relate to various segments of the image it is important to remember the information. By delving into the many possible questions to be asked about an image. You have to remember as many details as you can in the time frame available.

1. In the first place first, try to picture your parents' bedroom comprising a mountain range in the back, all with a brown paint. It might be high above their mattress and the middle of the mountains being the highest point.

2. It is possible to imagine your ceiling in your bedroom as an amalgamation of blue as a dominant color, and a touch to yellow (the walls may be sky blue or beddings could be blue or yellow with prints of yellow) to symbolize the blue sky of the picture and the setting sun.

3. Imagine that under the bathroom sink that there are boats as well on your floor you can see ducklings moving around in the river. How many ducklings are there on the floor?

4. It is possible to connect the items on the right side from your bathroom's left shore which might be the kitchen.

5. The left side of your bathroom may be your laundry room. connect this with the left side. If the laundry room isn't located situated to the left in your bathroom consider your confusion If it were. Add that feeling to your story.

Because these are places in your memory that you understand well, you'll quickly recall the various aspects of the picture. As easy as it is however, it gets easier when you are able to work at it. When you've mastered the basics then you can look for additional details in the image to help you remember.

3. Rebuild the Image in your Mind and then Construct it further

Once you've memorized the fundamental 5-10 elements of your image then answering any questions about memorization is straightforward. You must establish a link between the components of the image and the mnemonics that you choose to use. The visualization should be rich and include a mixture of reality and absurdity. The more memorable the scene you have in your mind's castle is the more easy it will be to keep in mind.

Chapter 9: Memory Techniques -

Names faces, names, and Numbers

Names and faces

The ability to recall names is similar to counting numbers. Just like people who mnemonize, can remember names and faces by taking the name of a person and linking it to their distinctive physical or facial features. While this may sound easy however, there are some issues, including:

* Can I immediately think of a similar word?

It is possible that after affixing the person's name with an affluent physical characteristic it is possible to recall his or her name simply by looking at their face or reverse?

When you utilize the body of someone to keep track of their identity, then the bodily characteristic employed is the trigger.

1. Select an appropriate Trigger

It is essential to select the trigger that must be a physical characteristic of the individual in question. Determine the physical feature of the person that you notice the most when you see him/her. It should be something that grabs interest in a distinctive manner so that you easily recall it every whenever you glance at the person. If you're unable to pinpoint an individuality don't be afraid to conjure up a fake characteristic, or highlight an unimportant aspect.

2. Choose a Mnemonic that is relevant and then Result

Be attentive to the emphasized syllables of the name of a person or word. In fact every word, even names are syllables that is highlighted.

Once you introduce it with the correct word, your brain is given the capacity to locate the correct word from the brain's pool of names and words in your brain. Below are some examples below.

Examples of Names:

Jessica

Sarah

Harry

Daniel

Brandon

Samantha

Ashley

I've picked these names since they are some of the most well-known names. It is evident that changing an accented syllable to an equivalent word or name is simple.

* J Yes I C

* S AIR ah

* HAIRY

* DAN iel

* B RAN DON

* Sa MAN the

* ASH LIES

Be aware of the syllables that are highlighted in red. These are the mnemonics that aid you to recall these names. When you speak the mnemonic, the appropriate name is immediately to the mind. For instance, if mention the word COAL your brain will instantly recall or register Nicole.

Since certain names are simpler to remember than others, you are able to be as imaginative as you wish. For instance, like the mnemonic of 'AIR "STARE" can be a reference with the word Sarah.

Analysis of the Name "Jessica'":

Name Name Jessica (the accented syllable you should apply in this instance is "YES").

Facial Triggers - You'll need to select Jessica's most distinct physical characteristic to serve as the trigger for her name. This could be her bangs when you call her. Again, if you are unable to identify a distinct aspect, don't hesitate to imagine a distinctive feature. In reality the more absurd the trigger is, the more likely this that the brain will not forget.

Mnemonic - Picture Jessica and her hairstyle in your head as she sighs in an up-and-down motionto indicate that she accepts what you're telling her. Her response suggests that you took the words from her mouth. She is eager to be with your opinion. Everything she does screams "YES!".

What you get from this is a multi-layered image that is Jessica in your head by nodding her head in a affirm what you're saying to her, and her distinct bangs bob between the creases of her forehead, hence her name is 'Jessica'.

For this technique to be effective for you, it is necessary to use it. When you next meet someone new, or make an acquaintance implement this technique in practice and be amazed by the results of your efforts.

Numbers

This technique for memory will assist you in remembering numbers. You should be aware that it's easier to remember places, stories or even pictures, rather than numbers since your brain doesn't operate in a way which makes numbers simple to remember. Therefore it is the most difficult for brains to remember because the entire concept number is undefined and only applicable to primates.

Example: 9192796512

Even though you may practice the numbers listed above to help you remember each number however, it won't work. How do we learn to remember the numbers? It is possible to group your numbers up into groups of three or four numbers, like this:

919-279-6512

If you break down each number string into small parts similar to what happens by telephone numbers, you could discover it easier to remember the string of numbers. Actually, breaking it down into chunks helps you to remember 'nine hundred and nineteen as opposed to the number '919'..

You can also employ the memory palace method and help to make it easier by connecting the numbers in chunks to the things your brain has been programmed to remember quickly.

Case Study:

Think about a memory palace consisting of just three locations, specifically The front entrance, the living room and the kitchen. It's all about creativity and connecting the bits of numbers to objects (mnemonics) that , when you look at them, you are reminded of them immediately.

Front Door Location 1

You exit the car and walk towards your friend's home. When you look up at the door, you see the address plate is '919'. It's been seen before but this time the chalky ceramic that the address plate is constructed from is strikingly visually appealing.

Another alternative is to appreciate the similarity of the number '919"' to '911' which is in America is the telephone number of police. You can also imagine how bizarre it is that the address of your friend's is so similar to '911'.

The Living Room 2nd Location

The number is 279; when you multiply 2 by 7 you will come up with 9 which is the number of the number. As you enter the living area you will notice that the living space is 9 feet tall and also has an chimney that's 7 feet high , and an imposing fireplace that is just two feet high. Because the chimney is directly in front of the fire place, their height is 9 feet, which is the total height of the living space. If you think about it you'll be able to imagine the charming living room with a two-foot tall fireplace, surrounded by the chimney that is 7 feet tall which is 9 feet in total.

The Kitchen: Location 3

The last digit "6512" could be related to your kitchen. As you enter the kitchen you will see a platter consisting of a dozen (12) eggs. The numbers 5 and 6 do not just appear similar (5 appears to be the number 6 which is broken) and follow one another in a numbering sequence.

Eggs are oval that is almost like the number 6. If an egg breaks, it takes on the form of the number 5 or more closely is similar to it. If you consider these connections by visualizing the figures, the chunk of '6512 will come to mind.

This is just one example of the numerous ways to help you remember this number sequence. This method is definitely effective but is a bit laborious. Therefore, I'd like to present an alternative strategy that uses the memory palace method, but is much more efficient.

The best method for remembering Numbers The Major System

This method will require an initial commitment of time. But once you've complete the required effort, remembering the numbers will be simpler than ever before. The result is amazing. We'll get right to it.

The procedure is straightforward it is as simple as taking the numbers 0-9 and assign a consonant sound each number. Then, we add two numbers simultaneously to make words. Here are the number-consonant pairs:

 (number): (consonant sound)

0. S (or Z 5:L

1 2: E or 6 J or SH

2 N 7: G or G

3 M 8: F or V

4: 9 A or P

Let's begin with a simple example: 15-32.

Based on the chart below:

1 = T

5=L

What's a word that begins by a "T" which is followed by "L"? An easy response can be "Towel". Be sure to select words that contain only consonants that are relevant. For instance"Towel" contains the "owe" portion of "Towel" does not have a number that is listed in the system of major. Therefore, I'm aware that the sole numbers that are represented in "Towel" is 1. (T) (T) and five (L). The simplest words work most effective as they are the easiest to remember and most likely have only two consonant sounds similar to those mentioned above.

3=M

2= 2 = N

What word begins by a "M" which is followed by "N"? The solution would be "Moon". We can see, time it's the "oo" portion of "Moon" does not correspond to any numbers on the chart of the major system. We know, therefore, that "Moon" does not correspond with 3 (M) or 2. (N). You can also utilize "Man" as well as "Moan". There are a myriad of words you can choose from. Make sure you choose only one word. When you are deciding between two words such as "Moon" and "Man" I would suggest that you select the word that is the most unique that is "Moon". The term "Man" is a bit ambiguous and may be confused with other generic terms.

15-32 = Towel Moon

To recall this simple sequence, go into your memory palace, and sketch an image in your head. For instance, you could imagine a scenario that you're using your towel to whip your way to strike the moon.

Let's take a look at a different example:

13-51-91-14-56-72

Divide the sentence into two pairs because this allows you to make simple two-consonant words. In reference to the list of major systems above, make a phrase for every pair.

1. (T) + 3 (M) = T-M = ToM

5 (L) + 1 (T) = L-T = LooT

(9 (P or B) + 1 (T) = B-T = Bat (I picked "B" but you could also choose "P" too.)

1. (T) + 4 (R) = T-R = TiRe

5. (L) plus 5 (L) + 6 (J or Sh)= L-SH = LaSH

7. (K or G) + 2(N) = K-N = CaN (The "Ca-" is the sound that is a hard "C" sound that is a sound that resembles "K". It is phonetic matches, not necessarily a match of letter-for-letter)

Tom + Loot + Bat + Tire + Lash + Can

Make a story right today:

It is your friend ToM is a burglar and begins to loot the store. If he is able to break the window, a swarm of Bats fly out. He rushes in to grab a gold tire. He goes out and is able to roll the tire down the street, creating a mound of eyeLaSHes. He turns and there's a little girl who throws an CaN to him.

In creating the story, and placing an emphasis on each of the nouns that is of interest, you will be able to quickly and efficiently "walk across" the story and determine the consonants that appear in the above nouns.

The more specific, odd or unique you tell your narrative, the better you'll retain the numbers.

How can you master the main system:

1. Create 100 small flashcards

2. Number them from 0 to 99.

3. Utilizing the internet as a tool or even using your imagination (which will be more individual) Create a new word for each pair of two-digits. Through the

process of learning numbers 0 to 99, you'll know every possible pair of two numbers.

4. Learn to memorize 10 cards every day. Within 10 days, will have this set memorized and you will begin to be able to recall the sequence of numbers.

Simply memorizing them doesn't suffice. As I went through this process , I believed that after I had memorized every combination, I would become master. But I was wrong. Every day you can create an unplanned series of numbers between 10 and 20 on your piece paper. Then, write an original story with your newly learned words. For 10 minutes, return and try to remember the sequence. You'll be amazed at how quickly you master the sequence. In the next few weeks, you'll be noticing that throughout the day you're identifying number pairs with their associated word. This can be made more enjoyable also "worthwhile" by remembering friends' phone numbers, pi digits, credit card numbers, etc. Also, anything that isn't random. Have fun!

Chapter 10: Memory Techniques

Poetry and Vocabulary

Vocabulary

Utilizing the memory palace method by focusing on stressed syllables, you will be able to learn vocabulary around 400% of your usual speed.

Using Emphasized Syllables

The brain can focus on stressed sounds, even without paying attention to the sounds. The trick to remembering words is to concentrate on stressed syllables , not focusing on the other letters.

You can also connect how a word is spoken with its meaning in hopes to master the concept. Similar to the rest of the material in this books, the deeper and more complicated your mnemonic becomes more likely you will be able to recall it.

Mnemonics

It is necessary to write something, it could be a narrative that connects to the meaning behind the word you'd like to remember. This means that you will not only retain what word you are using, but its significance. It takes time to associate the word with the story you choose and, before you realize it the word will be able to find its final place in your brain. At the end of the day, remembering the word will become automatic.

The Basis Model to help you memorize vocabulary

A story connected to the mnemonic's purpose is what triggers memory. Every mnemonic you create should be based on the stressed syllable of the word.

An Example:

Estar (Spanish verb that means "to be")

eSTAR

The stress syllable is STAR that you could use to say "I would like to be a star".

Syllables make it simple for you to choose the mnemonic you want to associate with your vocabulary. This means that every time you read a phrase or listen to someone say it, the mnemonic is brought to memory, which makes it simple to connect with the significance.

Make sure to practice as frequently as you can, and relish the process of learning the vocabulary. The most challenging part is the fun aspect and learning to appreciate the process is essential for your achievement.

Poetry

Traditional poetry is comprised of idea progression, meters and rhyme as well as stanza structure that make this type of poetry very interesting. In addition the rhyme and meter stay to the brain faster than other elements.

All you have to do is remember the poems' main elements, and then read the poem repeatedly and, in no time, the features mentioned above will make the poem stick to your brain like glue. Here's how you can recall the basic structure of a poem:

1. Recall the Stanzas with the help of Memory Palace

Usually, poems that have several stanzas address different issues within each. This is why you must link each stanza to the mnemonic you've stored in your memory palace, or a place you're familiar with. If the stanzas are excessively long you can reduce them into smaller pieces.

An Example: 'The Writer to Her Book' by Anne Bradstreet

The poem can be broken into four stanzas with each one having four lines. Then, you must link each stanza to the location of your memory palace. The palace should contain four places. You could choose to build play areas that have the wood platform and a ladder of metal underneath the platform, a steel slide that runs down to the wooden platforms and mulched ground under the slide.

2. Select One Prompt or A Keyword from Every Line

It is important to choose some words that will aid in recalling the specifics of the poem. This will also mean that you don't have to spend a lot of time trying to recall a lot of information at the same time. If the poem is long lines, take into consideration using two prompts for each line, but keep the same words throughout the poem.

The word you pick must be one that you are able to remember easily. The poem asks you to remember 24 words and 6 of them within each memory palace. You can choose to highlight the words, but you can alter them to one you find more easy to remember than the ones I have chosen:

Relate a word in each Stanza to a Memorable

The task is to link the word of the stanza with a place in your memory palace such as a children's playground.

A good example of Stanza 1

The word "offspring" can be compared to a small child at the bottom of the ladder.

He is there, hesitant to climb the ladder. It is this way until the other child on the ladder. The exposure to other children makes the child with a chubby body feeling very nervous and apprehensive because others look at the 'rags' that the child is wearing. In addition, the child wears a shirt with the word "errors" on the front.

It's about making up simple, but interesting tale that can aid you in remembering the meaning of the poem. While you are reciting the words, the meaning of the poem is not lost. The same is true for the remaining four stanzas.

3. You can think about your Prompts or Keywords

It is important to think about and test yourself on the selected phrases in each line. The more significant a term is simpler it will be to recall it.

4. Take a listen to Recorded Poetry

If you find a recorded version of the poem that you would like to learn, you can use it to read aloud to aid in recalling.

Once you've got the palace of memory set up it is easy to learn how to structure a poem, and then remembering everything.

Chapter 11: Memory Techniques
Texts and Passages

Passages

The First Letters of the Key Words

It is easy to quickly and easily remember passages with the help of their initial letters. This is true whether it's a chapter from the Bible or a brief speech, or a simple message to share with someone else. It is important to note that the key words you'll need to remember does not necessarily have to be key words or ones that are most frequently stressed.

Critical words are those you are able to easily remember.

A Case Study of a Insight taken from the US Constitution

Divide the passage into three sections:

1. The first seven words

2. The six defined purposes (highlighted)

3. Twelve words from the last 12 days

This technique will require you to remember the first seven words, and the last 12 words and the 6 important terms (purposes) at the center of the sentence.

The part that contains the 6 crucial words is as follows:

The 6 reasons listed into the acronym 'FEIPPS' to allow for quick recall. You can find a more simple term that rhymes if you'd like. When you think of the mnemonics you are able to connect it with the acronym, you'll remember "FEIPPS", and consequently the six words.

This is the most important factor to remembering difficult passages. Repeat the passage a few times with this method and observe how easily it is to keep in your head. The method that was discussed above for poetry could also be used for other passages.

Scriptures

The chapters and verses of the Bible make them simple to remember because they break it down into various sections. Utilize the following method:

1. Find the Keywords in a Verse.

An example:

It is possible to utilize the highlighted keywords to learn this passage of scripture. If you are able to remember the terms, they'll stimulate your mind to remember all the other words found in the text. Make a mnemonic tale, as mentioned in the previous chapter about the playground for children, in order to recall these words.

2. Memory Palace

You can learn a whole chapter with the help of memory palace, as I have described in the prior chapter. Choose one Bible chapter you like and apply the method using the method I described earlier.

3. More Objts

To be able to recall different chapters, you'd be required to add additional relevant places to the memory castle. This can be done for different chapters of the book, for instance, The Book of James. Each new place represents distinct chapters. For instance that you move from the playground to the cafeteria could indicate an entirely new chapter.

4. Many Books

If you are required to learn various books, you'll have to introduce an entirely new character or modify the memory palace.

Whichever method you decide to employ, keep in mind that different characters belong to different books; various scenes are correlated to chapters. Furthermore, each particular place in a scene is linked to a verse from the chapter of a book within the Bible.

Chapter 12: Methods to Enhance Memory And Thinking Biochemically/Through Diet

Water

Numerous studies have shown that drinking water may improve your memory. This is due by the simple fact drinking water helps you quench your thirst , and in turn, relieve the body from tension.

According to the research the researchers, drinking enough of water can improve your reaction speed and allows the brain to function properly.

In the end after drinking water and refresh your body it helps you to be more focused as well as think more quickly. You also gain clarity and greater creativity. Water is essential to survive. Make sure you drink more. You're sure to.

MCT as well as Coconut Oil

Coconut oil contains MCT (Medium Chain Triglycerides) fats. MCTs can penetrate the blood-brain barrier and supply the brain's tissues with huge quantities of energy. Additionally, their rapid absorption rates permit your body to use the energy more quickly.

A modern-day diet defined by an excessive consumption of sugars (sugar). While the brain's main fuel source is glucose (metabolized carbohydrates) and a diet that is high in carbohydrates can result in reduction in brain's capacity to transport, take in, and utilize glucose. This could be an explanation for neurodegenerative diseases as well as generalized brain fog. These symptoms show their symptoms as poor brain performance. That's where ketones come into.

MCT oils are metabolized into ketones, which serve as a second sources of power. Since MCTs are able to cross the blood-brain line, your brain makes use of ketones' energy source to operate at a greater rate than it did prior to.

Ginkgo Biloba

Ginkgo Biloba is Chinese herb which has been used for over 1,000 years. It is now one of the most popular herbs sold in America due to its ability to improve memory. Research has shown that extracts of the leaves of Ginkgo Biloba can improve or maintain the brain's social and cognitive functions. The root cause is an increase in cerebral blood circulation.

The herb is consumed in the form of tablets, tea as well as fortified foods as well as capsules. Be cautious when you are using these herbs because they are believed to possess blood thinner properties.

Pink Himalayan Salt

Pink Himalayan salts come up of pure salt crystals that originate from the Himalayan Mountains. They can be ground into powder and used in cooking recipes to give flavor and flavor to dishes instead of ordinary table salt.

The salt in its raw form is believed to be a natural source of iodine, iron, magnesium, potassium copper, phosphorous calcium, calcium, and chloride in addition to the 84 minerals that it has. Humans are in essence walking on salt water. The micronutrients Sodium and others are crucial to the actions that occur within the body. Thus, the proper dosage of the micronutrients are vital to ensuring proper central nervous system function.

Kale, Blueberries and Dark Green Vegetables

The research has shown that blueberries have flavonoid compound that can improve your memory and cognitive function, as well as reasoning and decision-making abilities as well as numerical capability, understanding of speech and ability to learn.

Additionally, the consumption of blueberries is believed to guard against Parkinson's disease and Alzheimer's and slow the loss of cognitive abilities.

Kale as well as other dark green veggies contain quercetin which is an antioxidant with anti-inflammatory properties that can help protect you from memory loss. The riboflavin vitamin-B compounds are able to protect you from migraines and headaches. Just a few advantages of these foods are being highlighted. The impact of eating a healthy diet are unimaginable. Similar to water, I'm certain you are aware that you must eat these foods. You have a reason: it enhances your memory. It's a good idea to do it.

Fasting (BDNF)

Fasting has the ability to boost brain activity through activating the mild response to stress. Research has shown that when you are fasting your brain releases greater amounts of BDNF (Brain-Derived Neurotrophic Factor). This substance has the capacity to stop the death of neurons in your body. Furthermore, BDNF promotes neurogenesis, which is the process of creating new neurons. In turn, neurodegenerative diseases like Alzheimer's disease are less likely be diagnosed.

Omega-3 fat acids

Omega-3 fatty acids, particularly DHA (Docosa Hexaenoic acid) are vital compounds that are beneficial to the brain's health and, consequently, improving your memory. The brain is comprised of the fatty acids. The higher intake of these fatty acids improves the effectiveness of your brain's functioning. This is the reason behind maintaining a healthy omega-3 - omega-6 ratio.

There are many sources of omega-3 fatty acids from fat fish such as tuna, blue fins, sardines herring, and salmon, in addition to algae and other fish.

Meditation/Mindfulness

When you practice the practice of mindfulness, you concentrate on techniques for meditation that focus on attention and a straight posture. It is important to pay focus on your posture, breathing and your thoughts. These are factors that are crucial in the general functioning. This is only one component of the overall puzzle to developing your brain's abilities. A focused, calm mind can remember things better than a distractedand chaotic mind. If you take the

time to do this, you can increase your
memory.

Chapter 13: Understanding How the Memory Works

It is vital to know how memory works , as this understanding will help us to go towards the right direction to developing our memory skills. There are three important components to memory:

* Attention!

* Storage

* Retrieval

Attention!

It is the act of focussing (concentration) on a particular aspect of something, while overlooking other aspects. The entire subject of memory and improving your memory is useless without discussing paying attention. To retain something, you need to be attentive at first. For instance, a vehicle could drive by, and you might not be aware the car; but you won't be able to recall the lesson a teacher gave during class, if you failed to pay attention in the beginning. So, in order to keep our memory intact, we need to pay attention. This could take the form of watching, listening or even looking for a mental image.

Storage

Your brain is a bit like computer systems. There is a short-term memory, also known as an active memory (more on this later) that functions in the same way as the RAM in computers in addition to an extended term memory that functions as the computer's hard disk. It's the job that the brain does to save the information it receives to ensure that it can be easily remembered when needed.

Retrieval

If you're unable to remember the majority of what you have kept in your brain, then you're not able to recall the majority of your abilities. Retrieval or recall is a major factor in memory. You can store data in an efficient manner however, it may be lost in the mass of other data. Consider a cabinet for filing with files that are kept in a state of neglect and without any sense of organization and another in which the files are organized in folders and properly maintained. Which one is more convenient to locate and retrieve data? Naturally, the answer is the one with the best organization.

The above scenario is applicable to how the information stored is later retrieved from memory. A well-organized memory is much easier to remember. This is why mnemonics techniques (more on this in the future) are being used to help improve the organization and presentation of information.

We have a good understanding of the three components of memory, let's be aware of the memory systems we have. Research has shown that there are three types of memory that comprise:

* Sensory memory

* Active or short-term memory

* Long-term memory

Memory: The sensory Memory:

This is the shortest-term memory. It allows us to store memories of the sensory experience that we have received from our sense organs even after the initial stimuli have gone away. The memory helps to store sensory information gathered from the five organs, including smell, sight and taste, as well as touch and hearing.

The results of studies have shown that the amount of time that sensor memory is able to store information is a small amount of time:

1 - 2 seconds to auditory information

150-500 milliseconds to display information.

The information that we detect with our senses may be deliberately ignored and, in that case, they vanish almost immediately. It doesn't require awareness and is completely beyond our control. The brain is designed to process information that could be useful in the future and also to allow whatever is remaining of the information to pass without being recorded. This eliminates unnecessary information , and allows to only the useful information.

The Short-Term Memoria (Working Memory):

The memory serves to keep information we're thinking about at the moment, so the name "working memory. Working memory's capacity is lower than the sensory memory, however the working memory stores information for longer that the sensor memory.

"As explained by the scientist Barry Gibb in his book"The general guide of the brain',"without the long-term memory you won't be able to identify who you are, where you are , or even the people you've met. Without working short-term or memory memory at the time you reached the end the paragraph you'd have lost everything I had said in the preceding paragraph". In reality, some of the information stored in the sensory memory gets transferred to the working memory in order for future use.

Although sensory memory doesn't require attention from a conscious person, working memory does require attentiveness.

Information is 'chunked' in order to increase the working memory capacity. Chunking refers to the breaking up of data into small pieces that are easily handled. Practically speaking, this means that when a person is studying or is trying to remember a particular piece of information, it is important to seek out and recognize an order to group the data.

"For instance, if someone is trying to remember an email address for a coworker (PR1990@gmail.com) The person will be able to remember and learn it quickly if they see an email address that is mixture of friends' initials (PR) and the year of birth (1990) rather than trying to remember six unrelated characters"

The above example applies to virtually every aspect. If you're looking to keep facts, always look for patterns and then use the pattern in your favor.

The Long The Long

The information is stored for an extended time period in the long-term memory. The memory of the long term can keep an endless amount of data. There are certain things you'll not forget. These things appear to be inscribed into your memory. This is the long-term memory working. Long-term memory defines the person you are.

Short term memories can turn into long-term memories via consolidation that involves meaningful associations and practice.

Chapter 14: Work Both Your Body and Brain

This is among the most effective ways to strengthen your memory, both sensory long-term, and short-term memory as well as your mental capabilities. A lot of people who are looking for methods to boost their memory forget the impact that exercising their brain and body can impact their memory. Learn how to make the most of exercises to boost memories in this section.

Physical Exercise

Regular exercise is a great way to improve your memory. If your oxygen levels are low, it becomes difficult to focus, making it harder to absorb new information or remember previous ones you've gathered. Regular exercise is important since it keeps the brain hydrated with the oxygen and glucose necessary for it to function effectively. The brain weighs only 2 percent of the body's weight, but it is responsible for approximately 25% of blood circulation and glucose.

The benefits and importance of exercising regularly were made clear during Australia when researchers published the results of a study conducted on 170 people who have begun to show signs of memory loss and decline. The participants averaged 30 minutes of exercise for six months. The experimental group scored higher in tests of their cognitive abilities as compared to the controls. The reason for this is that physical activity increases growth factors and produces new neural cells in the hippocampus which is among the most important brain regions for memories and for learning.

The hippocampus's shrinkage that is a brain region that is involved in memory formation, was believed to be a result of aging, however studies have proved that this is not the case. Studies have proven that performing moderate aerobic exercise can not just stop shrinkage, but also reverses shrinkage after an entire year.

It might be difficult to keep up with your workouts even when you work at a full-time job or working part-time, especially with more kids to take care of or you are in a plethora of classes. However, it's important in knowing that 30 minute walk every day can help focus and clear your mind. to focus more effectively. The point I'm trying to make is to take advantage of every opportunity to work out your body.

ACTIVITY

Set aside an hour or more each day to do physical exercise. You can do it in any manner that is suitable for your needs. It can happen during the morning or in the evening. It can take the form of jogging, pressing up, walking or running or walking, etc. It is important to workout every day for minimum 30 minutes.

Exercise Your Brain

Your brain is just like every other body part in that you need to work your brain to maintain it top condition. Many people are great at fitness, but neglect training their brain.

There is a thing I always do. It's simple, but it works. When I'm confronted with tasks that require me to think for a long time and with a lot of effort I reach for my smartphone and play some of my favourite games. My most played games are brain-teasing games. Here's the way it works is relax my muscles and stimulates the brain.

Here are some suggestions to exercise your brain that will provide immense benefit to you:

* Play daily crosswords

* Play chess

* Read books daily

* Play video games that require the use of

* Daily brain teasers for the brain

* Read newspapers daily

* Play Sudoku

* Complete educational courses

"Remember this that even if you are retiring physically, don't let your mind go to sleep. Research has shown that keeping up with the ability to think and be active throughout life may keep memories in check even into later life."

Brain Stimulators

The brain is the place where all the data gathered through the sense organs is processed. Do you recall your last experience when you were able to see something intriguing and delicious, or ate a tasty meal and received a sound that was amazing? These events that can stimulate (wakes the) our minds. It is important to keep your mind active every throughout the day.

ACTIVITIES

Make sure you expose all of 5 senses stimulating things every day. You may be surprised to discover that your senses will be more sensitive as they once were.

Try these suggestions:

On sound:

Find out more songs

Spend more time listening the sounds of nature

On the visual:

Find more movies

Review your photo albums

Take a trip to the sights

On touch:

Enjoy a relaxing bath

Make sure you are checking your skin temperature regularly.

Taste and smell:

Just to enjoy the experience

Try some new dishes

Prepare your own favorite meals or go out to eat.

Chapter 15: Food for the Brain Fuel for your Brain and Memory

The kind of food that you consume can influence the way your brain works. Certain foods aid in improving brain function. Nutritional health is important to nourish all body parts system, including the brain.

Certain food items are often called 'brain food.' The term was coined because of their capacity to directly or indirectly influence memory and the brain. They help protect the brain by releasing antioxidants, which are chemical compounds that help break down the harmful chemicals (oxidants) which your body naturally produces. They also contain nutrients and vitamins which are vital to the general health of the body.

It is important to note that obesity can lead to elevated blood pressure, which reduces cognitive performance So, make sure to be aware of your weight. Adequate nutrition, however, can help prevent cognitive decline.

Be aware that whatever is beneficial for your brain can be beneficial to your memory. Be sure to eat breakfast regularly because studies have proven that those who skip meals (children and adults included) are not able to perform well on tests at school as well as at work contrasted with those who ate their breakfast. A healthy diet is essential to ensure the proper functioning of your body, therefore always consume a balanced diet and take your breakfast.

Below Are Some Dietary Guidelines that will help your memory:

Water

Your brain gets hydrated with water and is crucial that your brain remains maintained. The lack of energy from drinking water can affect your mental health and may affect your memory. Drinking water can also improve your recall abilities, as per research. While it's not as funny as it might seem, UK researchers believe that students who drink water throughout exams perform better than those who do not. One reason for this could be that the students have a moderate condition of dehydration during their exams, and this can be corrected by drinking water.

Healthy Fats

They help build the brain. They are plentiful in soybeans, fish as well as walnuts, eggs, and fish.

Fiber

They regulate the supply of fuel throughout the body. Fiber assists the brain in performing at its highest level. Sugar is a source of energy that the brain needs (glucose is not sugar refined). Fiber is a key ingredient to ensure that sugar is slowly absorbed in the bloodstream. Foods that are high in high levels of fiber are beans, nuts seeds, fruits, vegetables and more.

Antioxidants

They protect the brain by creating chemical compounds that clean the brain.

A few brain food items that are recommended are as follows:

* Apples

* Green and spinach

* Vegetables

* Onions

* Avocados

* Legumes

* Eggs

* Green Tea

* Dark Chocolate

* Bananas

Your brain requires a constant flow of glucose to work properly, so steer clear of food that can increase blood sugar. Avoid foods that contain white flour. Also, avoid soda since it delivers an excessive amount of refined sugar into your system all at all times.

Make sure you get enough sleep; it helps your memory

Numerous studies have proven that sleeping improves memory. The brain needs about 7 to 8 hours of sleep per every night. Sleep deprivation can affect the brain's ability to process information, and also weaken long-term memory. It may also cause mental instability.

Have ever wondered what makes you feel refreshed and relaxed following a relaxing night's sleep? The reason is that sleeping calms your mind and aids in the brain to function more effectively.

If you're studying this book as a student and you are a student, take note of:

Students are often forced to sacrifice sleep in order in order to improve their learning and memory however the opposite is also true. I'm not advising you to read at night. What I'm telling you is to establish an appropriate balance in your learning routines. Make sure you get enough rest. Studies have shown the transfer of information to long-term memory when we sleep. Therefore, we tend to retain information that we have studied prior to going to sleep more.

But, I'm not suggesting you abandon your efforts to master your skills at night, but do I suggest that you are important to review what you have learned before you go to bed, and the most important thing is to include enough sleep in your strategies for improving your memory and productivity.

Check That Stress

The effects of stress on the brain cells and can affect memory. In stressful circumstances the brain can be weakest. Stress and information overload tend to weaken the brain further. The prevention of stress and managing stress is vital. Monitor your stress levels and review your work load. Reduce it as much as you can as well as outsource and delegate when you can.

Memory loss among older adults is believed as being related to excess production of cortisol (which is typically released during stress situations).

Neurologists are also of the opinion that memory loss in older individuals is mostly due to stress and not due to the advancing age.

In the end, laughter decreases stress hormones, such as cortisol or adrenaline, so don't treat yourself too seriously. Find things that make you feel happy and laugh more often since it lifts your mood, improves your think more clearly and boosts your memory.

Chapter 16: The Reasons Why Do We Forget?

Most people have at one moment or another experienced the feeling of the effects of forgetting and how it affects us. It is vital for us to comprehend what causes us to forget as the main purpose behind memory enhancement is to decrease the speed of forgetting information. Therefore, the main question is: why do we forget? Could it be because the information that we stored in our memory is gone? Perhaps it's because it's been altered or lost in our brains? Perhaps we didn't master it at all? There are many theories that have been proposed and plenty studies have been conducted to understand why we forget, however the first comprehensive attempt to explain and understand the reasons of forgetting was created by Hermann Ebbinghaus. His study and later ones showed that forgetting is rapid initially, but it is gradual as time goes by. We will now examine the various theories proposed to explain the reason we forget.

Trace Decay

The argument is based on the assumption that memory triggers changes within the brain's central nervous system, which causes physical changes in the brain known as memory traces. The memory trace are, however, merely fade out when they aren't employed for an extended period. However, this theory has been proven to be ineffective on a variety of grounds. For instance, I've already stated previously in my chapter those who fall asleep after having memorized are more likely to remember than those who remain awake after learning. This, therefore does not support this idea since the memory trace is not used while one sleeps, however people remember more when they is asleep after having memorized.

Since this theory is unable to provide enough explanation for forgetting, a different theory was developed in lieu of it. The new theory has gone quite a ways to explain the phenomenon of forgetting, as it suggests that the introduction of new information into the memory can interfere with the recall of information that was previously stored.

Forgetting As A result of Interference

Interference occurs in the event that a piece of information is into the way of other (similar) piece of information. It is thought that memorization and learning are the process of making an association between different data points. Once the association has been established the information is in the memory. over time we are able to acquire additional similar information in the same way through such associations, however each is stored in a different way. Interference is a problem that arises during recall, when the various groups of associations are competing to be retrieved.

Maybe you can grasp the concept of the concept of interference with the simplest practice.

Create two lists of random syllables. List 1 and list 2. Have a person take 10 minutes to study and remember those syllables. After a few minutes, ask them to remember the syllables from list 1. If he/she cannot can't recall the syllables in list 2, that's due to the association formed while studying list 2 is hindering the association formed when studying List 1.'

The types of interference are of interference: retroactive interference and proactive interference.

Retroactive interference happens when new information blocks the recall of old information. Retroactive interference occurs when you attempt to remember a password from the past to an account , but only remember the present password.

Proactive interference On the other hand it occurs when the older information is unable to recall new information. For instance, you may experience this when a friend moves out of town and alters their phone number. If you dial to the previous number you're experiencing an active interference. Failure to remove (forget) outdated information could hinder the memory of new information. For instance, it could be extremely embarrassing to accidentally calling your girlfriend or boyfriend with your previous lover or friend's name.

Forgetting due to Retrieval Failure

It can also occur when the cues to retrieve (these aids in helping us remember information we've learned) are not present or ineffective when recalling information.

This is usually the case when we have a lot of memories associated with one trigger. For instance, if you need to keep track of Peter's cell phone numberas well as his spouse's cell phone number as well as his office phone number, as well as his home number, we'll be less effective in retaining them all, like we would be if we only have to keep his cellphone number. To summarize, Peter is the retrieval trigger, and if we connect a lot of memories (four as in the example above) to Peter, we are less effective in remembering them all.

Since we've gotten a better understanding of the reasons behind forgetting, it is essential to implement certain techniques to prevent forgetting, or at the very least, decrease it significantly. It is impossible to highlight the issues without providing solutions. The suggestions below can contribute to reduce forgetting and increase your memory

* Try to limit interference

Interference is among the most common causes of forgetting , and it is important to try as hard as you can to stay clear of it. If a lot of related materials or information are studied in a series that results in maximum interfering, which is why you need to avoid this. Plan your learning in such as to not study relevant information one after the other, but rather study unrelated material one after another. If that isn't possible then you can spread your learning by taking breaks at intervals so that you don't get interrupted.

* Design Retrieval Cues Enough for Yourself

To increase your memory and prevent being able to remember, you should offer a variety of cues to retrieve information for yourself while studying any material. While you're studying new materials look for retrieval cues within the material, and connect areas of the content to these cues. These cues will be easier to remember and the connections you make between these cues and other aspects of the content will help the retrieval. "A important factor in improving memory is to increase the amount or quality of the retrieval cues."

"Thomas and Robinson came up with a new method to aid students in retaining more information. The steps are : Preview Reading, Question, Read Self-recitation and Test. For a preview, you must look over the content to become acquainted with the content. Questions are raising questions and looking for answers within the course. Start reading the lesson and respond to the questions you've asked. After reading, you should revise what you've read for a while , and then you can test your understanding of the subject to see whether you are able to comprehend what you've learned."

Always Be Engaged In Deep Level Processing

Engage in deep-level processing if you wish to master something and increase your memory. Beware of surface learning as it is a study technique that is passive which involves repetition and repetition (rote memorizing). While it may seem to make it easier and quicker to remember information over a short period of time but when it comes down to the application of knowledge and higher levels of knowledge, they are unusable because they consume valuable period of time which could otherwise be better used for deep learning strategies.

"Craik Lockhart and Craig Lockhart have proven that processing information related to the meaning they convey can improve memory contrasted to paying attention to their superficial attributes. Rote memorization is often the cause of long-term memory that is not connected and significance. Deep level processing however is aware of associated information, and its connection to what you already are aware of. This way, new information is incorporated into the information you already have, thus increasing the likelihood of recalling it."

For deep-level processing, you must follow the steps listed below:

* Participate in Retrieval Practice:

Ask yourself questions and then answer them, because every time you use memories, you build it. Self-tests help you pinpoint your weak points and increases your ability to remember the information in the future.

• Take a break from a lecture or reading to review what you've learned

• Explain what you've learned to others. The act of teaching others is the potential to increase your memory and knowledge on an area of study.

* Label and draw diagrams that you can recall from your memory

* Rehearse New Information Elaborately

Link new information the information you already have. Learn the details and connect it to your previous knowledge.

* Think of common examples that you can connect to

* Rephrase definitions and descriptions using your own phrases.

Make Space for Your Studying

Instead of taking on a certain topic for a long time of 10 hours, it's more beneficial to spread your study into five two hours or ten one hour sessions or two five hours of sessions. Spread your learning over multiple days. Examine the information you would like to remember each day.

Chapter 17: The Use of Mnemonics

Mnemonics are widely used as a key memory enhancement technique. Nearly all methods for improving memory are dependent on the use of mnemonics. A simple method of remembering information in a short time is recording the information with clear mental images that are simpler to remember. Mnemonics are strategies employed to aid the brain retain information. It could comprise an acronym, song or rhyme.

Rhapsodies and jingles can be quite catchy and easily memorized. Sometimes, it's impossible to get the lyrics out of your mind. An excellent example is "30 days consist of September and April, as well as June and the month of November'. By using this rhyme, you'll not forget the months that have 30 or 31 days.

Mnemonics are utilized to aid memory. Let's take another illustration. A majority of people are unable to comprehend the difference between stalactites versus stalagmites. Stalactites are suspended from caves' ceilings and stalagmites grow from the floor up. The task of identifying the distinction between the two terms could be difficult if you do not improve your memory.

How can you improve remember this instance? Examine the terms carefully and stalactites contains an 'c' located on the last syllable of its second, whereas stalagmites contain the letter "g.' It is possible to take the 'c' in stalactites as represent ceilings as well as the 'g' of stalagmites to mean 'ground', so that any time you come across the two terms and you'll know that the one with the letter 'c' is hanging at the top of the cave while the one with the letter 'g' is derived out of the ground. This can be a method to aid your memory since it's much simpler to remember these terms by this method. The same technique can be utilized in any situation to boost the speed of memory.

For creating powerful mnemonics I'll provide you with three fundamental principles to help you:

* The Imagination

This is how you can use to create powerful memory aids. Human brains are capable of amazing imagination. the more you can imagine and imagine a scene and the more you can stay in your mind in order to remember the information later.

* Association

This method lets you connect a piece of information to something else that is more easy to remember. In this way, you can connect details you'd like to keep with the information you already have to help you remember it. This can be done using various methods, including:

* Affiliation using the same color or shape or scent and so on.

* Images that link to each other

* Adding one data over another

* Location

This creates a consistent framework to put information in a way that it is hung together and differentiates one mnemonic from another.

Mnemonics by using the Images Method

In order to use mnemonics using images, you need to create vibrant and relevant images that represent the information you'd like to keep in mind and remember quickly. Two distinct methods of mnemonics utilize images. They are the method of loci as well as the keyword method.

*The Method Of Loci

The details you'd like to retain will be arranged sequentially in a physical space as visual images. This method is very effective when it comes to remembering things in sequential order. It is necessary for you to first visualize the items you want to remember and then associate them with physical places. For instance, if are trying to remember salt pepper, tomatoes and salt when you go towards the store, then you can imagine a mental picture of salt sitting on the dining room table as well as pepper and tomatoes on

111

an utensil in your kitchen. In order to ensure that when you go at the store, all you need to do is take an imaginary trip along the path from your dining table, to your kitchen, and you will remember the items in your list in order. This method is useful in any circumstance that requires you to recall details in a sequential order.

In a nutshell the loci method includes these steps

* Visualize the information or items you'd like to recall

* Assign familiar physical places to these items

* Create a mental memory of these physical locations and you'll be able to recall your belongings.

* The Keyword Method Keyword Method

This technique involves linking an 'keyword' to what you wish to remember. For example, if you would like to recall the word the word 'pato' (which refers to the Spanish word meaning duck) You could select the word 'pot' as your keyword, and then create pictures of that keyword as well as the desired word (pato in this instance) in a way that is interconnected.

To facilitate For convenience we could imagine an image of a duck sitting in the water in a pot. In this way, when you think of an image of the duck, it will will quickly recall the Spanish word that means duck.

Mnemonics using the Organisation Method

This is a method of placing order on the information you want to remember. This makes recall simpler. Certain strategies can be employed in order to get this organisation:

* Chunking

Chunking is the process of arranging items into easily manageable units. It increases the capacity of short-term memory. However, to create blocks, it's essential to find the organizational principles that connect smaller units of data.

* Acronyms and The First Letter Technique

Acronyms are words composed of the initial letters in a sentence, or any information you would like to remember. Acronyms are widely employed to retain information after they have been been transferred to memory for long-term use.

You can change your information into words or acronyms, or even a single word or phrase, and arrange it in such a manner that it can be retained to create your acronym.

Other common acronyms include:

PIN is Personal Identification Number.

ASAP - as early as is possible.

Chapter 18: Memory Improvement Techniques 1

Preparing for a Memorization Session

Technique 1

Make a Space In which You Are able to Work On Your Practice and Memorize

You can complete your studies and memorization wherever you want in the bus, in the streets or anywhere. However, it is beneficial to have a distinct space that has been mapped out to allow for extensive study and memorization. The space you choose should be relaxing quiet, peaceful and free of disruption. Create a space that excites you, and make it cozy enough for memory. Sitting on the ground next to the bookcase is inspiring and excites you, then make the space to write your notes. If it's at the table in the dining room or the garden, you can use it to help you remember your thoughts.

There is typically a strong relationship between the activity and where you are engaged in the event. It is more comfortable going to a soccer field to play football rather than playing in the streets; it feels more appropriate going to church for worship. It is more comfortable going to school for learning in a different way than elsewhere. There is a connection between the sport and the place it takes place. Profit from this connection to create a special place for yourself where you can study and recollect your knowledge.

Technique 2

Set a schedule for your Memorization

A routine will help you concentrate and keep your focus. Being consistent with a schedule can yield amazing outcomes. If you're a musician trying to perform an instrument, you may stumble and then have to begin over. This is a time-consuming process. However, when you break down the piece into parts and study the parts that hinder you from progressing You then attempt to perform the entire piece. Similar principles is applicable to memorization.

The way I approach it is I go to three daily sessions lasting 30 minutes each day. Consider your memorization to be a meal including breakfast, lunch and dinner. It may sound strange but it delivers amazing outcomes. It is possible to start at any time you like, and will gain experience as you go along. Don't limit yourself to just 30 minutes, however I suggest 30 to 50 minutes of sessions.

When I need to remember something, I just sit down and unwind. Relaxation can help reduce cognitive resistance and improve your creativity. In addition, I think of something interesting about the material I'd like to learn. Consider what memorizing of that content will allow you to achieve, and let the result you imagine will provide the energy to improve your motivation and enhance your rest.

Technique 3

Learn to Access the material

Also, you should begin your memorizing sessions with the simple portion. You can begin by learning something simple and easy at first. It will boost your confidence and motivate. It doesn't matter how difficult learning the information or material it is always a angle that it can be considered to make memorizing process easier.

Be on the lookout for these more relaxed angles and slowly ease into the subject. You could also learn an easy and short thing that doesn't concern the main thing you're trying to master at first. Footballers will always run and warm up prior to the game, pastors will prepare his sermon prior to the congregational service. A person who is a memory keeper could also warm up their brain prior to studying!

Technique 4

Be Prepared for Mistakes

It is perfectly normal for you to fail. It is not necessary to comprehend or master everything on the first go around. It's real that the aim of memorizing is to become perfect, But remember that anything will not be able to stick in one sitting.

Don't get discouraged when the information you're trying to master or remember isn't sticking quite well. Relax. Relax. Take a deep breath, then return. Sometimes, you'll not remember something you've learned a few minutes back. Trust me when I say that it's normal. Relax and try again until you are able to do it the right way. The point is that even while we're striving for perfection, let room for errors. Do not give up for a mishap or because you've made numerous mistakes.

Technique 5

It's OK to Try another Method

Sometimes , you'll spend hours trying to remember something by using a specific method and then you realize it's hard to remember. It's okay to abandon the technique and try a different one. For instance, you could try to recall facts using the loci method but you find that it's difficult to remember after several attempts, instead of having to spend more time trying to improve it you can try a different method, like the acronym method.

Do not spend your moments trying to figure out how to make one technique work, when you could test out different methods. I am not suggesting that you be rushing from one strategy to the next without giving the previous one the best chance. I am merely informing you to be innovative and active. Be aware of when to stop and try a different approach

We are always reluctant to give up something we have put our time and effort into; we would prefer to put in the effort, time and energy to make it successful instead of letting it go. However, I'm telling you today that if your system fails repeatedly, don't waste time with it. Instead, take the time you invested in it as part of the test-run process and begin fresh with a different system.

Technique 6

Be fit and stay healthy

The importance of regular exercise and a balanced diet is emphasized in the second chapter, but it's of great importance to remind yourself that in order to be able to remember effectively, you have to be fit and healthy. Your brain needs to function at its maximum and your entire body to be fit and healthy. Exercise regularly, eat healthy and remain in shape. It can be extremely beneficial.

Chapter 19: 20 Specific Memory Techniques

Learn these methods and play using them to create strategies that best suit your learning style. The techniques for memory I'll demonstrate in this chapter have been tested and praised over the years by experts in memory. To make the most out of this chapter, you must go over the methods by first studying the chapter's headings and then studying each one attentively. Choose those that suit you most, the ones you like , and work using them.

These techniques are divided into four distinct sections. The three first categories deal with comprehending and effectively storing information. This is likely where the most memory battles are decided or not. I am convinced that you'll prevail. The four categories now are:

* Arrange the data:

It's much easier to locate organized information, the first step would be to organize any details we would like to keep so that it is easy to be found.

Engage your body in the following ways:

Every sense should be involved actively in the process of learning.

Use your brain:

Your memory is strengthened during the process of learning.

* Get the details:

This is what we are trying to achieve with memorizing, to recall what we've learned. This is simpler when you follow other methods successfully.

ORGANIZE THE INFORMATION

Technique 1

Be very selective of information

There's something known as information overload. Avoid drowning in details. You'll always be bombarded by hundreds of facts and information about a specific topic. You don't have to be able to recall all of it.

If you're in school, for instance while studying your textbooks, you should carefully identify the most important points to master. Avoid drowning yourself in facts that will not be relevant in the end. Check out summaries, review questions chapter previews, and take note of facts and statements that are boldly written. Pay attention to the visual elements such as graphs, charts, or tables. Take note of anything the instructor stresses in lectures. It is a good idea to assume that you will create test questions based on the content you're studying. Also, decide on the type of questions you'd like to be asked. This will assist you in separating information in a proper manner and select the most crucial aspects that can aid in your comprehension of the subject.

Technique 2

Use the information to make it meaningful

The best method to make information more relevant is to identify the central concept. Each piece of information, be it book or journal, presentation, or others, always contains an idea at the heart which all other information is built on. Take a look from a broad view to a particular one.

To make it easier for information to remember, you should arrange any list of items in a meaningful manner. Use the guidelines below to organize any type of information.

Sort by Alphabets: for instance, how entries in an index to books is listed ABCD order.

Sort by Time such as novels always take place in a chronological sequence

Classify your library materials by category: for example, library material is classified into categories such as non-fiction, fiction, etc.

Organise by Location: for example, addresses for banks' branches are classified by state and city.

Technique 3

Establish Meaningful Associations

Information that is already in your memory is arranged in a manner that is clear to you. When you discover new facts, they will be easier to recall it when you connect them with similar data already stored in your memory.

If you're in school, many of the courses you take at the university will require prerequisites. Knowing the prerequisites can assist you in understanding and recalling the new subjects since the information you learn will be instantly linked with the knowledge you already have. The courses you like most are likely to be related to a subject that you already know a bit about.

If you are looking to gain knowledge about a new topic it is helpful to build up your background knowledge of the subject since background knowledge is the basic basis for a meaningful association. Students will notice that they comprehend the subject better when they have read their notes before taking classes. Everything you need to master is an update of previous knowledge. Establish the connection between the information you already have to improve your memory.

It is also possible to create association by connecting thought to an object or an image so that when you think of an image you will remember the details. A master speaker, Cicero employed this method during the 60th century BC. He would write his speech and practice it as he moved from room to room. He would practice different parts of his speech in different rooms so that when the moment came to deliver his speech, he just imagined his home and then repeat what he had practiced.

INVOLVE YOUR BODY

Technique 4

Take Action

Don't just read, do something! Moving is a fantastic memory booster. Use the techniques for memory you are taught and identify which ones work best for you.

Instead of just thinking about these methods take action on them.

Participate with your whole body into the process of learning. Sit up and study or walking back and forth using hand gestures or reciting the material loudly. You can sit up while you are studying. In general, you should involve your entire body into the process of learning.

Technique 5

Relax and enjoy the moment.

This method may appear to be in contradiction with technique 4. However, it's not. Relaxation means to feel comfortable, calm and alert. It's a state of not feeling stress and tension of any nature. It is possible to be active and relaxed.

It's much simpler to learn when you're at ease. Your mind is able to play with new information and make connections easily. Stress is extremely poor for memory. A lot of times, students forget what they did not understand in the exam, but they can repeat the same sentence following the exam if they're calm. Be sure to remain relaxed while learning new information.

Technique 6

Use Images

Make use of your imagination, create images that reflect what you're learning, and then use them to make associations that can assist you in remembering the information. Create cartoons, diagrams, or illustrations, and use them to connect concepts. It's simpler to remember the things we see, make use of this for your benefit. To effectively visualize abstract connections make sure to use images that are action-packed.

The brain part which is responsible for visual information is distinct than the brain that process verbal information. This means that when you make visual images of an idea, you're putting the concept in a different part of your brain, which helps you remember it.

Technique 7

Sing it loud and repeat

This method has been around for a long time, and is extremely efficient and powerful. Two senses are involved when you speak something out loud. You feel the sensations on your throat, tongue and lips as you speak it. Also, you can hear it. Make sure you recite any facts you would like to remember loudly If you are able, don't repeat it in your head unless it is in a library or an event where you are unable to recite out loud. The ability to recite it in your head is fine, but try to repeat it as loudly as you are able. It's simple, but extremely efficient.

Recite the recitation repeatedly. Repeat the recitation until you are sure. Repetition of information creates pathways through your brain, which helps you remember the facts. It is most effective when you're using yourself as the source of information. When you repeat the information you wish to remember with your own personal words and you have to think about it this way, and you will remember the information faster.

You'll have a lot of enjoyment with this method. There are a variety of ways you can repeat and recite details. You can compose an entire song about it, and perform it anyplace. You can apply this method everywhere and it's easy fun and enjoyable.

Technique 8

Make Notes (Write it down)

This is an simple and effective method that is often overlooked. Notes you make for yourself can help in more ways than you think of, even if you never get to read the notes over and over. Notes on ideas make the thoughts more efficient, organized and cohesive.

It is also possible to apply the method of repetition. Record a specific idea over and over again. As you write your arms, fingers and hands, as well as your brain are all involved. Keep in mind this is the case with learning. It's an ongoing process.

Another benefit of writing thoughts down is that they uncover the gaps in oral reviews don't as oral reviews reveal gaps that written reviews don't. Writing helps you organize your thoughts and helps you to be more rational while taking the information into your mind.

Make use of your brain

Technique 9

Utilize Your Emotions

There is a part of your brain that increases the activity of your neural system whenever you experience an intense emotion. This brain region is known as the 'amygdala.' This part of the brain in order to improve your memory. When a piece of information triggers any kind of emotion, such as fear, love, hate or laughter, the amygdala transmits signalling to your brain to indicate it is important and must not be lost.

This strategy is a good one to try even if you find the topic boring. Take whatever steps you can to create interest in the subject matter, establish an emotional connection to the subject matter , and connect with the subject matter more emotionally. When the topic has a connection to a purpose, it will trigger emotions in you, making it easier to recall. Make goals that are specific about the goal you are aiming for because by doing this you will create new pathways within your brain to receive information.

Technique 10

Do More Research

Do your best to discover what you desire. Examine the subject matter take your time, research it deeply and ask yourself questions. study more, study it until it is a part of your. Discover more than you want to be aware of a specific area.

This method is effective for solving problems. If you're studying for an exam such as a test, then go through the book thoroughly and then solve the problems assigned or consult other textbooks to solve similar problems. Make up problems by yourself and work on solving them.

Make sure you test yourself like you were writing the test already. It requires effort and patience but the results are always amazing. You'll become more precise and confident.

Technique 11

Transfer them to your long-term Memory

We've already figured out how long- and short-term memory functions. It is possible to glance at a number and keep it in your mind enough to call it, but then forget it within the following two minutes. Therefore, you will always need details that you can keep in your memory for the long term.

It is imperative to avoid the trap of short-term memory by reviewing what you've learned. Review what you have learned within a matter of minutes or hours after remembering it. This helps in shifting it into your memory for the long term.

Technique 12

Make Use of Your Times of Peak Energy

Everybody has a moment that our energy levels are at their peak. It could be early in the morning, later in the evening, or even during the middle of the day. Pay attention to those peaks and valleys in your energy flow continuously and alter your study time according to your current energy level.

It can be beneficial to learn the most difficult elements of a piece of work in these periods of peak energy. There may be flashes of memory power at certain moments of the day. make sure to take advantage of these times.

Technique 13

Make Space for Your Study Time

Spaced-out, shorter sessions are more effective than lengthy continuous hours of study. This technique is very effective as it improves memory. It is possible to accomplish more work accomplished in just three sessions rather than a three-hour one.

Let's suppose that you are preparing for an American exam in history. Study for about two or three hours and then give yourself an opportunity to take a break. It is possible to use the break to chat with a friend or even clean dishes. While you're working, your brain is still reminiscing about American history. You can return to your study for about an hour, then take a break. You could play games, listen to an instrument or even go through your emails. It will give the brain some time to rest, and can aids in absorbing the knowledge you've acquired.

Be careful not to overburden your mind with many ideas. It is beneficial to divide your brain in a variety of ways. You could even use breaks as mini-rewards. This reward might be allowing yourself to go through your social media accounts, make your friends and play with your kids or even play games.

There are also times when you don't feel needing to break, when you're completely absorbed by something that you are not like taking it off or being so obsessed with the idea that it's all you could think of If you are in that situation, then continue and have fun.

Technique 14

Take a look at Your Attitude

This method is similar to technique 9 , where you need to utilize your emotions. Many people believe it is difficult to learn Mathematics is difficult struggle to remember mathematical equations and formulas. If something does not agree with your view and you forget it. People who believe that the past is difficult to remember remember have trouble remembering dates.

If you find a subject that is boring to you, try finding an opportunity to link the subject to another topic that intrigues you. You should develop an interest in the subject. Don't just study it to learn, but bring it into your own mind and you'll never forget it. Be aware of your attitudes to a specific area and try to change an attitude that blocks your memory.

Consider, for example an individual who loves automobiles. He can build an automobile in a day and enjoy a great moment doing it. He is also able to investigate a variety of knowledge thanks to his passion for automobiles. He is able to connect the working mechanics of an engine to physics, mathematics, and the study of chemistry. He is able to study the automotive industries and their impact on the agricultural and business.

In the above example, you can see how one's car-related interest is connected to other fields. Therefore, in any subject you'd like to know that's boring, try to find ways to connect with something that you find fascinating. This will make learning the subject interesting to you.

Technique 15

Avoid Retroactive Inhibition

Psychologists define retroactive inhibition as an event that occurs when new information disrupts previous knowledge. The actions you do after learning can affect how you remember the information later on.

Consider, for instance, that you've just completed an introductory lecture in psychology. while driving to home, you have a conversation with your classmate about the lecture and the conversation leads to a discussion in which both have different opinions. When you return back home, it's likely that you reflect on the discussion that you and your classmate had and connect it to the major aspects of the lecture you took. This will assist you over time to recall the lecture. However when you've discussed something completely different with your classmate during your way to home the topic that you talked about could hinder your memory of the lecture you attended.

Technique 16

Combine Memory Techniques

These techniques for memory work better when used in conjunction. Choose two or three methods and then work on them. Test them and weigh the outcomes.

Combining techniques can engage your senses of touch hearing, smell and taste in the process of memory.

You could, for instance, sketch a diagram that represents the central idea of a book after you have a general overview of the book. You could also discover a mathematical equation by creating a jingle of it and then singing it in order to learn. You can also spread your studies in short intervals.

READ the information

Technique 17

Keep in mind the information related to it

There are times when you think you are aware of something however you are unable to remember it. You can try to think of an equivalent event. ask questions to aid in making more connections. For instance, when meet someone you've never met before consider asking yourself: does the person you meet remind me of another person? If the person you meet recalls someone else you are more likely that you'll be remembered when you think of the person that he is a reminder of.

If you are unable to remember the name of your great uncle Try to recall the name of your great aunt. If you are unable to recall particular information Try to recall the lesson the instructor taught you. Also, you can brainstorm ideas to boost your brain. If you don't remember a question during an exam, note down a variety of answers to the same question. The answer you're looking for might pop up.

Technique 18

Pay attention and notice when You Recall

Each of us has our own capacities for memory and different styles. Certain people can remember the things they see more easily than reading, and others remember their actions effortlessly. Be aware and think about the type of memory strategy you utilized to recall information quickly.

Be aware of times the times when you are having a difficult remembering details and record the strategies you used. Utilize relevant information to improve your memory strategies and praise yourself for getting better.

Technique 19

Make Use of That Information

I am sure that you are able to remember your current telephone number, but it'll be very difficult to recall your phone number from 10 years ago, would you say? This means that in order to constantly remember information, it is necessary to be able to access it frequently. Information that is stored in the long-term memory should fade when it's no longer used.

To be able to remember information, it is necessary to read it, talking about it, and then applying it.

Another method for getting information is to teach it to others. When you share your knowledge with others they don't just know more about the subject but you gain more knowledge by observing other's perspectives. It is also possible to participate in study clubs. This helps you utilize the information in a way that you are less likely to forget the information.

Technique 20

Take a positive attitude that You Will Never Remember

Sometimes, the attitude of a person is all important. Stay clear of negative thoughts. Instead of saying "I do not remember,"" tell yourself "it will appear to me." Instead of saying "I have a poor memory,"" tell yourself "I recall information quickly." Utilize optimism to boost your memory improvement. A positive outlook can always lead to growth by providing you with the enthusiasm and energy needed to improve your memory.

Chapter 20: The power of associations

The methods of association utilize the brain's capabilities. The brain is extremely strong and is able to store information for a long period of time in the event that the information has been stored in long-term memory. When you connect new information to what you already know it is simple to remember the information. An outstanding public speaker Cicero used this strategy during the 60th century BC. He would write his speech and practice it as he moved from one room to the next. He practiced different elements of his speech in different rooms so that when the moment arrives to deliver his speech, he just thought of his home and repeat what he had practiced.

Great Aristotle was recognized as the author of Four laws on association. A number of memory systems are built on these principles.

1. Contiguity is a law Similar to how the computer memory keeps your browsing

history safe and links events that happen near one another. When you browse your history, it is stored by dates. Your brain also saves data that you have accumulated over the course of a specific time. For example, if you go to the place you were raised and born in the past, it triggers memories of various events that happened in the time you lived there. in the event that you are near the river, you might remember the moment you nearly drowned in it, and the list goes on.

2. The law of frequentity: When the events of two or more are regularly associated, the connection becomes stronger. For instance, if, for example, you've always had bread and tea for breakfast for the past 10 years, then every time you think about tea, you will be reminded of bread. Additionally, when you consider breakfast you'll at the very least consider bread and tea.

3. Similarity is a law Similar information is kept close to one another within the brain. If you are thinking about your pet, for

instance it is possible that you are thinking about your friend's dog too.

4. The law of opposites: For example the thought of an exam that you failed can cause you to think of the exam which you did very well on.

Visualisation and Storytelling

Experts in memory say that the majority of people aren't trained in memory and not necessarily bad memories. It is possible to develop your memory to be all you desire. The brain's capabilities are unlimited. Your brain enjoys hearing stories. Stories can help you see information through your eyes. Visualization is an extremely powerful tool for memory that you can make a connection between various things in your head and while creating the connection, you're also creating memories in itself.

The information that you imagine in your head is usually simpler to remember. The more vivid the picture that you make in your mind's eye, more likely you are of recollecting it. When you combine visualization, storytelling , and conscious association, you will create strong memories that are quickly recalled in the future. While you look through the pictures below, try to imagine it in your head. Think of ways to be creative and innovative.

Imagine that you must remember these ten cities of the U.S.A. in the order shown below. The method we will employ is a combination of storytelling and visualization to help you memorize this list.

1. New York

2. Los Angeles

3. Chicago

4. Houston

5. Philadelphia

6. Phoenix

7. San Antonio

8. San Diego

9. Dallas

10. San Jose

The first thing to do is browse the list. You should be familiar with the cities, not worrying about the order currently. The next thing to do is to make the image you have in your mind to aid in remembering the first city. Then, connect it to the next city and so on.

For New York let us pick the symbol of New York (the statue of liberty). Imagine the liberty statue in arms, in the direction of the torch and angels carrying the torch. Be sure to visualize the image in your head and bring action to it. Angels should be moving around with their wings flapping. When you attempt to recall the first city where you can are able to see the Liberty statue that represents New York. You also observe angels passing the torch. "Angels" provide the essential clue for you to recall the second city , Los Angeles.'

Then continue to develop the story by thinking that the angels hold white chickens that are trying to walk into a home. The chickens will bring back memories of the city that is next, 'Chicago and the chickens trying to get into a house will remind you of the city of Houston.'

Continue to build the story and making connections until you reach the final city on the list. Make connections that are clear and dramatic, and continue to review the story until you have committed the story to your memory. Keep reviewing the story, and, if you do stumble, begin again and ensure that it is a permanent memory in your mind. The unique benefit of telling stories and associations is that once the story is anchored in your mind you are hardly able to forget it. It is rare to forget an item from the list because the story connects to them all, unlike the case with memorizing by rote. If you learn the list in order one after another without any sort of connection, and you accidentally forget one of the items in the list you will likely will not remember the additional items listed or you lose their positions within the lists.

Chapter 21: Learning to Prepare for Exams and Presentations

I will employ the methods of storytelling, words and association to demonstrate how you can easily break down a piece of material for examination or presentation, then to learn and remember it easily. If it's an item list as well as a speech that you need to present or material to be examined that you wish to remember using the technique of storytelling, keywords and association will never let you down. The more you practice these strategies, the simpler and quicker they will become for you to use them.

The technique of analyzing keywords involves reviewing the material and identifying keywords that can give you clues that will aid in remembering the entire information. Once you've picked your keywords and you are able to apply the method we employed to recall the 10 cities in the U.S.A. (that is storytelling and association technique).

Imagine that you have to remember seven leadership styles that demonstrate the degree of trust and engagement among employees. Assume that you receive the following explanation from your instructor or lecturer and then required to write it down on an exam later in the day.

1. A manager who makes an announcement of a decision without any form of advice or input from employees. Similar to a dictator, or tyrant.

2. A manager who makes the decision to make it and then explains the decision to the entire group without input from employees, but explains to them the reasons behind the choice is the right one.

3. A manager who takes questions from staff members but makes an individual decision. Staff's opinions are not taken into consideration, however there is an underlying sense of participation from the employees.

4. A manager who takes an unconfirmed decision but takes the final decision after talking in conjunction with his team. The

team is involved in the decision-making process.

5. A manager who presents the issue to the team, relying on the suggestions of the team before making the final decision.

6. A manager who can explain the issue to the group and agrees with any solution that they propose.

7. A manager who instructs the team to work within the set limits and makes choices as the work progresses.

The words I highlighted are the key words I've selected to in creating a story to assist me in remembering the seven styles of leadership. The story will reveal the key words which bring back to you of the various leadership styles. You then explain them using your personal words.

Let's Visualize This Story for Illustration:

I am watching an announcer speak to a crowd of people. I note down the word "announce" while thinking of this. The next step is to think of what the announcer would be saying. He's announcing an event which will take place on the day of tomorrow. I also write down the word'sell.' The crowd starts asking the announcer what's available for sale, and he says "tents, tents are up being offered for sale.' The word"tent" makes me think of the word 'tentative', so I write it down. Continue to build the story by imagining what might happen within the tents. Then, I see presents set up inside the tents. I quickly note down the 'presents.' I then see a bunch of people trying to get the present to take as much as they can. I record "group.' I think to myself, what is happening in members of the group?' begin to cooperate well with everyone taking care of his or her own business. I record "work".

Keywords are now listed in the list. is:

* Announce

* Sell

* Questions

* Possible

* Present

* Group

* Work

After the story has been saved to memory, whenever I need to recall the seven different styles that lead, the only thing I have to do is follow the mental process of reciting the story. write down the words and my brain will fill in the gaps. It is possible to add as many details as you can in the story to make it exciting and engaging. You'll be amazed at the amount of information you can recall with this method. All your brain will requires is some help in retrieving the information in your long-term memory.

However If it's a speech you're planning to prepare for, you should outline the topic and sub-topics you'd like to discuss connecting them to a story similar to what it was with the 10 cities of the USA. It is not necessary to memorize your entire speech since you will obviously you will be speaking about something that you are familiar with. The fact that you have a list of the most important things you're planning to discuss will ensure that you won't forget everything when you're overwhelmed by stage fear. Be sure to review the stories you've created to engrave them in your mind and to make sure that the memory isn't fading.

Chapter 22: Recalling Names and Faces

It's common that people have difficulty remembering names at one time or another. However, it is possible to reduce this to a minimum level when you adhere to the guidelines I'll be sharing throughout this segment. To fix a problem it is necessary to identify the root of the issue first. When you have trouble remembering someone's name, it might be because you weren't looking to commit this name in your permanent memory at all or you didn't remember the name correctly. It could also be because there isn't enough associative data to help you remember the name quickly in the future.

To overcome the challenge of not remembering names or faces of people begin by deciding to take an interest in the lives of other people. Your brain is aware of your desire to keep things in mind and, when it is aware that an item of information is significant to you, it becomes easy for the brain transmit the information to your memory for the long term. Be open-minded and relaxed whenever you encounter new individuals. and repeat the name of the person repeatedly in the course of conversation. Associate facts with the people you meet and attempt to picture the face of the person in your head in the future. Make use of the ability to associate your brain. Similar to how the Liberty statue is a reminder of this city called New York, a person's face will bring back memories of their name if you establish an emotional connection. This can be done by identifying a distinct facial feature like the eyes, the nose, the mouth and so on. And then, mentally link that specific characteristic to the person's name. If you come across the person again (that particular feature you made note of) will aid in remembering the name of the person through the association.

Let's consider an example. You encounter someone at a gathering named Billy. You examine his face to identify one particular feature. You choose the ears of his, likely because they're larger than the normal. When you speak to him, you change your name to that can and say "billy goat.' You create an picture of a white goat emerging from his ears. Keep in mind that whenever we created stories, we have made the stories dramatic and exaggerated to ensure that they are more easy to remember.

When you get to meet another person, say two weeks after, you look at for the person's face and then ask yourself what the most distinctive feature you picked. It's his ears. What is happening to his ears? White billy goat is emerging out of his ears - the name is Billy.'

It might seem confusing and complicated however it's not. The objective is to produce something that helps you recall the name and face. Some people have difficulty converting names into tangible objects and are also unable to discern an identifiable feature. However, in the majority of instances, the simple act of looking at the person's appearance is enough since it could be permanently engraved in your mind and just need a little suggestion to be remembered.

Don't be worried if you find this challenging, as it will get easier as time goes by. Keep the clues short and clear; it will work always. If you are able to identify the name as "Henderson" and you pay focus on the face of the person and try to recall it later the only thing you have to do is visualize an 'hen' resting upon the face of the person (maybe the head). If you see the person again, after your brain has the clue "hen," the complete name "Henderson" will be brought back from your memory for a long time.

EXERCISE

Learn the names in the following list and practice using them as clues that can help you identify them later:

Mike Bush

Robbie Pitt

Donald Lemon

Lorena Cherry

David Stinson

Anne Smith

Terry Gunn

Change each name into something tangible, that sounds similar to the name. Then , visualize the object and attach it to a distinctive facial feature. It's always a good idea to keep it simple and re-read the image as often as you're able. The most important thing to remember here isn't the image that you envision, but the effort you put into it because , when you attempt to do it you're attempting to look at the person's face and their name with a keen eye and also to connect with the person's name something tangible.

Let's now pick alternate clues to the names that were listed in the above exercise.

Mike Bush: Microphone can be used to portray Mike, Bush is okay.

Robbie Pitt Robbie Pitt is near Robbie and the peach pit is acceptable for Pitt

Donald Lemon: A donkey eating a huge Lemon upon his forehead

Lorena Cherry Arena be used to make Lorena and cheese may be used to make Cherry

David Stinson: visualize David fighting Goliath sporting a large Stetson

Anne Smith: Ant for Ann and blacksmith for Smith

Terry Gunn: A teddy bear with a gun.

Do you get the concept? Connect a tangible object that has a similar sound to your name with the person's face. Don't get discouraged as it becomes easier as you get better at it and also helps you more attentive to the faces of people and names that are so easy to forget.

Simple Rules to Remembering Names and Faces

Many people have difficulty to connect names and faces to tangible objects, as

I've described above. If you're in this situation, don't worry just follow these basic guidelines and your capacity to remember name and face will increase more than ever before.

1. Motivation is among the factors that contribute to having a great memory. Therefore, put in the effort and choose to recall people's names as well as faces for every person you encounter.

2. If you're being introduced be attentive to the name of the person and pay attention to hear it clearly. If you are unable to hear it clearly then request someone to repeat the name.

3. Repeat the names when you hear it, and try to repeat the name as many times as you can during the conversation. For example, you can say "It's a pleasure to be with you Jane following the intro.

4. Take an active interest in the people you're talking to and keep the focus on them, not your own personal interests. Discover the most they can on them. It will help you to have plenty of things you can

associate with them, allowing you to remember the names of their faces and even their name quickly.

5. Take note of the face of the person and note the distinctive features like eyes or noses, mouths or mouth. Try to connect the features with something else, but do not worry if you are unable to achieve this. It's all you require.

6. Note your names down of the people whom you encounter. Think about them while writing the names down. The names you write down will make them more permanent in the long-term memory. You can keep a notebook to keep track of this and revisit it frequently.

7. Make a plan before you are meeting with a large number of people at an event or party. Be at the right the time to introduce yourself to everyone one by one. After you have met a few people take a break and look over the names and faces of the people who you have already met.

8. Practice then practice and repeat. Apply these methods to your daily routine and

get in touch with the maximum number of people within a single day.

Chapter 23: Remembering Telephone Numbers

The Game of Numbers

The majority of people struggle with to remember phone numbers or hotel room numbers, as well as other numbers that we come across daily. If you're naturally adept with numbers, you might not require this method. If a number is often used, they are transferred to the long-term memory. However, numbers that are not utilized often take a long time to learn. The numbers are harder to recall since they do not create any visual images.

But before I proceed I'll say that the best method to keep track of numbers is by noting them down to be able to use them to reference them at all times. When you're in an office or a restaurant don't try to remember the information when you could just write it down. However, if you have to remember crucial numbers, you can utilize the memory system for numbers that I'll explain.

Certain numbers can be divided into smaller pieces that are easy to remember. For instance, 94847464 could be broken into 94-84-74-64. These two-digit numbers are gradually decreasing by 10, which makes easier to remember. A bigger number such as 1960101520 could be broken into the 1960 (a number of years) and 10- 20 (2 number of digits growing in 5).

One way to be sure to remember any number is to translate them into objects or words that are easily visualized. In order to do this, we'll use the code we'll remember in the near future. This may be difficult initially, but the advantages are huge. I'll also provide some tips for memorizing the code.

The code we'll use has each number between 0-9 that is represented by the sound. These are:

The sound of's", or 'z' comes from the word 'zero.'

One of them is the sound 't''d', or "th.' It's easy to remember this by considering 't' and "d" as having just one stroke down.

2. The sound of "n.' "n" has two down strokes.

3 The sound of'm'. "m" has three strokes down.

Four The Sound of "r". "r" is the final letter in 'four.'

5 . The sound "L.'

6 . The sounds of "j'"g," "ch or'sh'. J appears to be the reversed version of 6, and you may be able to remember it in this manner.

7. The sounds of the letter 'k' or "c'" (when used to describe "cat")

8 Sound of the letter 'f' the sound similar to the letters 'ph' and 'v.'

9 The sound of 'p' or 'b.''P' appears like reflections of 9. So you'll be able to remember it this way.

Be aware that all letters are consonants. Letters such as h as well as w and all vowels will be used to serve as fillers without any meaning. Make note of the code above before reading further.

The effectiveness of this method is contingent on your ability to learn the code. Test your self repeatedly until you can master the code completely. What's the number three? It's a'm'. What's the matter with number 8? Learn to study them until you can recognize the order of them, and then read on.

To further illustrate Let us change some numbers into meaningful words that we can imagine. 43 is the sound of 'r' as well as'm. This is a way to make words like 'room' and "ram.' There are a myriad of words that you can make use of, but be aware that vowels do not mean anything. They're only used for fillers.

Also, 901 is the sounds of "p" or "b" as well as the sound of's or 'z', and sounds of the letters 't' and 'd'. It could be represented with using the terms 'past' "boost," and like that. Be aware of the fact that vowels are fillers having no significance. Also, keep in mind that double letters represent only one number. For instance, the word 'batter' can be used to represent the number '914' and not '9114'..

EXERCISE

Form words derived from the following numbers by using our code number:

15 ....

98 ....

150 ....

4567 ....

67432 ....

4325 ....

Be aware that you don't have take your time trying to make one word from any number of numbers. It's okay to make more than three terms, and then link them. Try this method by making phone numbers into groups of words, and see how it is easy to keep them in mind. The applications you can make use of this code to do are endless. For example, if you wish to remember this number (921-2975) you can create a word like "paint knob cool" or any other expression. You could make it a link to the person who is the person painting an entryway knob.

The system for memory of numbers is extremely effective for long numbers after you have mastered the algorithm, as you can quickly connect phrases or words into a narrative that will stay in your mind for the rest of your life. It is easy to remember the social insurance numbers the driver's license or insurance number, and easily remember them without having to find them out of your pockets!

Remembering Statistics

To convert statistics, just change the numbers into words, then connect them to make the story. Avoid decimal marks in the event that they are included. Your memory and sense of smell will inform you of which decimal point to be when you convert back to numbers from words. In order to be successful at memorization it is essential to be proactive and imaginative. Discover ways to make use of your memory strategies you've learned.

Let us suppose that you wish to recall the increase in productivity net over the past 10 years. You can convert those numbers into words in the following manner:

Year Net Productivity percent Clue words

2000 1.5 tall

2001 2.0 nose

2002 4.1 Rat

2003 6.5 girl

2004 8.2 oven

2005 12.1 dent

2006 15.0 dolls

2007 17.4 tiger

2008 18.0 doves

2009 21.4 nectar

You are able to select different words. There are many to pick from. Be sure to select words that you can easily visualize and then connect them to create an interesting story. Then, practice using the words mentioned above, then use the words to tell an outline of a story. See how easily you remember the data.

Chapter 24: Memory The Good The Bad as well... The Last One I forgot the last One

If memory is this amazing yet it tends to be a failure? When I had to manage the various tasks I mentioned in the past, I was not sleeping much. I was tired often, which impacted my health. Many people today have the same issue. Sleep plays a major role in memory. In those precious moments of inactivity (from your point of view) your brain is at work , trying to organize all your memories throughout the day. The information you find valuable is stored through strengthening connections between neurons in your brain (called neuronal cells). The rest gets discarded. There's still a place for it inside your mind, though the odds of recollecting it are low to zero. But, if you'ren't having enough sleep (at at least 8 hours) this process hasn't been complete, and you could lose important information. In addition, once you've fallen into a habit of sleep deprivation and you begin to feel like "you're okay with it" but you aren't aware of the consequences. This is why your memory declines more because you're constantly stressed and distracted.

Sleep deprivation is just one cause, however. Memory is also at risk if you attempt to master too much in a small amount of time. One of the biggest mistakes I made as an undergraduate was believing I could remember entire textbooks within a couple of weeks prior to my exams. Most of the time, I'd perform well however, I could never actually remember all the information I needed to know. I was over-stressing my memory, and making it work to process thousands of pages within one or two weeks. Whatever the skill level of the brain's abilities are such things it will need rest. After a couple of hours of study it's hard to remember any information anymore. This is the reason why studying for hours produces much less results than the majority of students realize.

Consuming a lot of caffeine or sugars can affect your mental performance by default. It's called default because while sugar and caffeine are known stimulants but they also leave your mind in a state of disarray. Sugar triggers blood glucose and insulin levels, to increase, which causes an insulin deficiency later. So, after the "high" has gone away then you'll be at the "low" and you require more to keep going. It's an adrenaline rush. The same is true for caffeine. The effects of caffeine are temporary but then you begin fighting withdrawal symptoms (yup that breakfast "pick me up" isn't really stimulating you , it just brings you back to a normal level). In reality, caffeine is the reason why you require to drink in the first in the first. It's an endless cycle.

These are just a few of the most frequently cited reasons your memory may not be the sharp it could be. We'll go more detailed in the methods for improving memory however for now, it's important to consider the damage you're causing for your brain. I didn't know how much of this affected me until I stopped drinking coffee, cut down on sugar, and began to sleep frequently. It was a struggle to do it but after you've made it through the first week, it becomes much more manageable. Personally it started out as an "fun" test. I wanted to test how I could get rid of the sweets and caffeine but be able to get to work. It was a struggle initially however, a few days later , I realized that I was feeling better. I began to sleep more deeply and feeling more energetic, and didn't require stimulants any more. I replaced my unhealthy habits with healthier alternatives. The coffee became peppermint tea. Sweets were replaced by oatmeal, bright fruit and veggies. I started exercising because I felt great!

If you're trying to improve your mental capacity, then the initial step is to stop sabotaging your own efforts. I understand the reason you do this, as It was me in the exact situation not long back. However, it is important to realize that the immediate satisfaction you get when you eat sugar or drink coffee isn't worth the cost. If you get more sleep and eat a balanced diet and train regularly, you'll be much more relaxed overall. I'm sure that you're squinting right here, and I'm unable to convince you to do something that you're not eager to do. The only thing I can say is that it's worth the effort therefore it's worth a give it a shot. In the end you'll still be able to reap the benefits of methods we'll be discussing in the future chapters, but making the smallest changes in your lifestyle, no matter how difficult it may be, will certainly improve everything, not only your memory.

Chapter 25: Practice Makes Perfect

Being active, eating healthy and getting enough rest seems like a good way to beginning. If you've been able to implement some of the changes to your life that you made in the previous section, you'll have begun to notice some improvement already. If you've made the decision that you're not ready to quit coffee or sugar, then you'll begin to notice changes after this chapter. However, you've made it this far, so we've going.

The ability to remember can be improved. There are various routines and exercises you can develop to increase your memorization and attention skills in everyday life. The good thing with this exercise is you are able to practice it anyplace and at any time. One of the exercises I found to be particularly helpful was watching the cars that walked by on the road. Because I'm always late (or at the very least in time) so I usually end in waiting for my buddies. I have 5 to 7 minutes (on average) to improve my mental capabilities. What I'd suggest is to observe the cars passing by and try to recall all the details of every one of them as possible: color and model, the license plate, sticker, obvious flaws and so on. By doing this, your brain is told that you must be aware of something and it's more easy to concentrate and stay focused. When I first began I was able to remember only a few details about each vehicle I passed. If I was able to remember the colors and models of three vehicles that was quite an accomplishment. Nowadays, I don't have to think about it, it's automatic. I am able to easily recall the details of more than six or five automobiles and hold this information for a long time. The best part is that this has made me more aware in general. If you teach the brain to become more attentive and attentive, you will soon realize that you're much more focussed on the present and you're also more alert to the things going on. You are more aware and can remember more since your mind isn't "scattered" all over the place.

This easy exercise is suitable in any situation. For example, you could attempt to remember the clothing of the three people you've saw on the streets (just not stare, or people might think that you're creepy). Try to memorize the cereal orders at the grocery store. This doesn't require moving however, you must be sure not to spend too long otherwise it will fail. It shouldn't take more than 10 minutes. If you fail to remember it in the first attempt Don't be concerned about it. Just try it again later. It will happen eventually and you'll notice the way your memory overall will get better. However it is important to be cognizant about that "use it or you'll lose the memory" rule. It is important to maintain this level or else your memory will return to the old capacities.

Learning the ability to learn (and be sure to remember, having a good memory is a talent) requires dedication, time and practicing. When you work out and become better, however you'll be more determined. It's similar to when you first start exercising or try the latest diet program initially. It's hard initially, but when you begin to see the outcomes, you'll continue because you're eager to do more!

The process of improvement also requires good habits. You must constantly work on your memory to improve it. One of the best ways I've learned to do is trying to recall random information I've read on the internet. This has helped me improve my memory and enabled me to participate in nearly any conversation or conversation anywhere I go. Being able to know a lot (but having no need to be a guru) is an excellent opportunity to meet new people and increase your social circle. But, you don't need to be a pro even if you don't like it. Your habits could be more practical-oriented for example, such as keeping track of names, numbers names, etc. without having them written down. It can be difficult initially however, you'll become proficient at it. When it becomes routine, you won't need consider it, you'll automatically remember more details.

Another good habit is to work to improve your mental focus. Most of the time, people don't consider the things they do, and in reality, don't even think about the things they think about. Our thoughts aren't monitored throughout the day. This is the reason you may put your keys in the washer and go looking for them for a half an hour after you're ready to leave. It's not really your intention to think about what you're doing because you're focused on other things. Learning to become more aware will assist you in that regard. Instead of just throwing keys around you can develop the habit of putting them down in a thoughtful manner. Don't do it just for the sake of it and forget about it, but consider it. When you place the keys down. Take note of the location in relation to their position, and everything else. This is only just a moment however it can make a connection with your keys as well as the location you've left them. Consider other things that you typically do not think about. If you lock your door, consider closing the door. If you are leaving your car at a particular location be aware of the place you'll be going to leave it (make sure that you don't connect it with any other vehicles as they may be moving). These few minutes you'll spend to observe what you're doing could save you many hours later. It will be necessary to think about it at first, but , like other routines, it will become automatic. Develop your mind to be more conscious The only thing you'll forget is the fact that you've been in a state of forgetfulness.

Conclusion

Stress isn't good for memory. Go in the direction of your flow and don't be confused by the strategies in this book, or by the numbers code. Remember to write down things and keep a record of them. Always exercise your brain to improve your mental abilities.

Pay attention to particulars and details you want to keep in mind. Stay in control of your actions, only do only one thing at a given time control stress effectively and manage technology well; do not allow technology to control you.

Get enough rest, eat properly and take part in activities that bring satisfaction. Maintain a vigorous lifestyle throughout your retirement years. Take advantage of the things you are able to do, and forget about the things you can't accomplish. Keep your mind focused and positive, and you'll get positive results.

Always refer back to this guide after having read it first time. Continue to practice the techniques and improve your skills.

www.ingramcontent.com/pod-product-compliance
Lightning Source LLC
Chambersburg PA
CBHW060330030426
42336CB00011B/1276